"In a world where the consequences of thoughtless
actions reverberate far and wide, understanding
the intricacies of human behavior becomes not just
a pursuit of knowledge, but a necessity for navigating the complexities of our society."

- Jones -

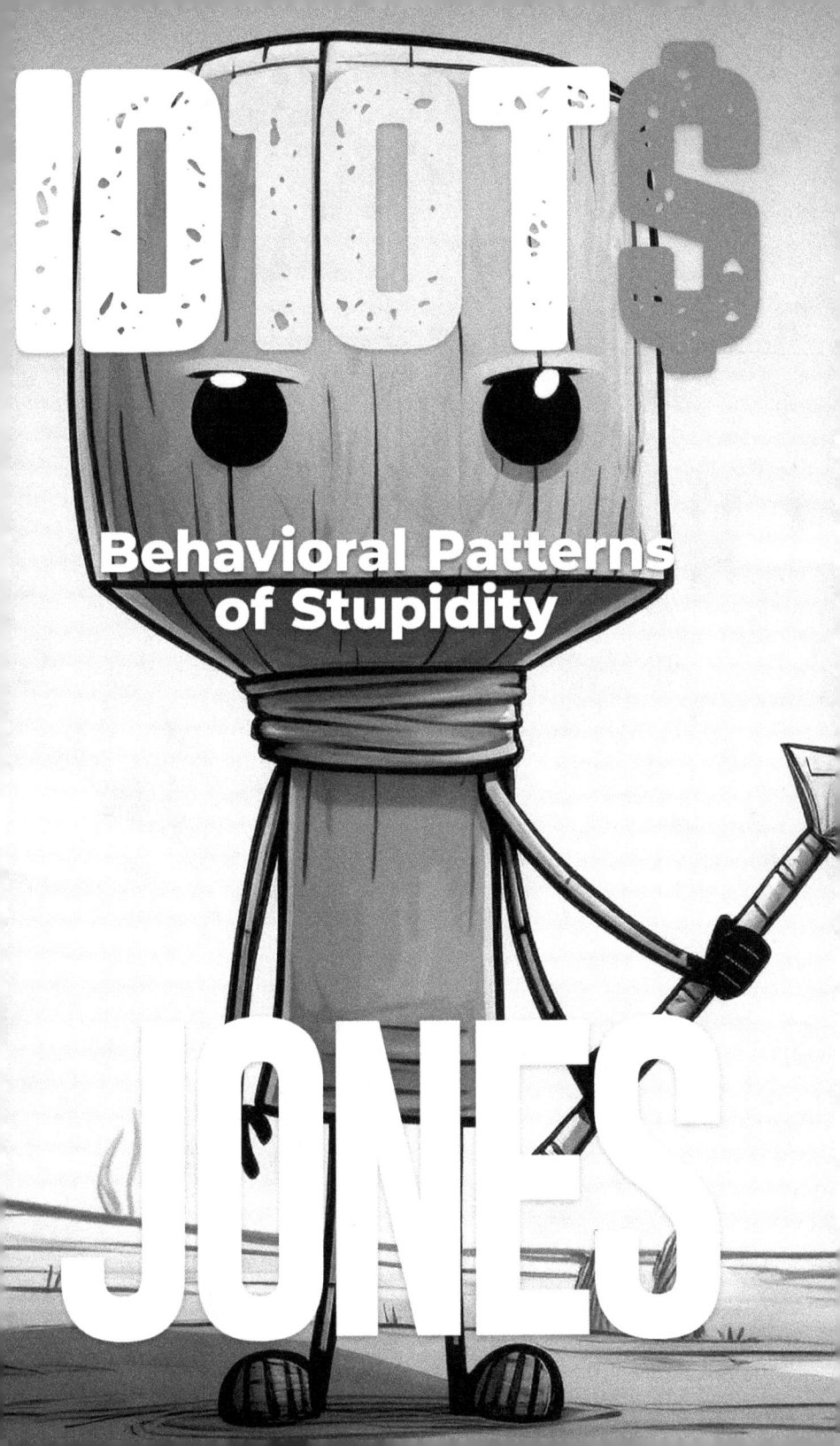

ISBN 978-0-9763065-8-0 (paperback)

Book Cover and Inside Art by Cyphur + Art & Design

To Nija and Gisele,

Amidst a world where ignorance frequently holds sway, both of you radiate as pillars of intellect, empathy, and resilience. This dedication stands as evidence of your steadfast dedication to pursuing truth, confronting falsehoods, and aspiring towards a brighter future.

As you journey through life, may you continue to embrace the noble pursuit of knowledge and understanding. Never underestimate the power of your voices to combat stupidity and ignorance, whether it is through education, compassion, or simply leading by example.

Remember, true enlightenment is not just about acquiring wisdom for yourselves but also about sharing it with others. As you navigate the twists and turns of life, may you find opportunities to gently guide and rehabilitate those around you, nurturing their minds and hearts toward greater awareness and enlightenment.

With love,

Dad

Contents

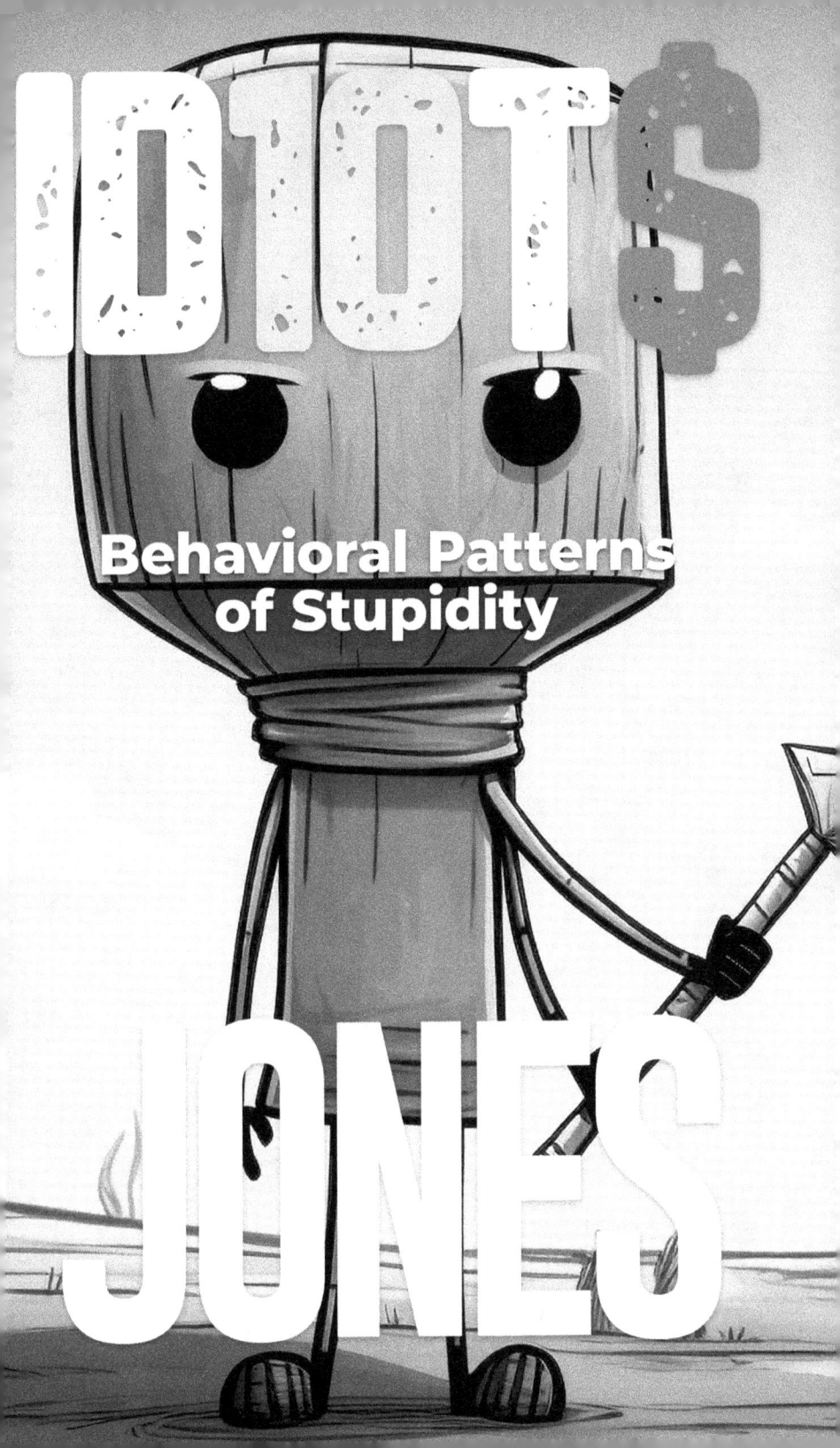

IDIOT$

Behavioral Patterns of Stupidity

JONES

Foreword

Stupidity is an ever-present force in our world, manifesting in countless forms, often masquerading as humor or harmless ignorance. From cringe-worthy mistakes to catastrophic blunders, we've all witnessed and perhaps even perpetrated acts of pure, unadulterated foolishness. We've encountered individuals who consistently defy common sense, leaving us bewildered, amused, or sometimes exasperated. It's tempting to label them as "idiots," "morons," or, in the digital age, "ID10T$."

The prevalence of stupidity is a topic that we must address, not with disdain or judgment, but with understanding and compassion. In a world increasingly driven by information and intelligence, recognizing the behavioral patterns of stupidity has never been more crucial. The purpose of this book, "ID10T$: Behavioral Patterns of Stupidity," is not to mock or belittle those who display such behaviors but to shed light on the complex web of factors that contribute to ID10T moments.

Stupidity, in the context of this book, encompasses a wide range of behaviors, thoughts, and actions that can be described as moronic or foolish. These behaviors, far from being confined to any particular demographic or social group, permeate every corner of society. We encounter them in our workplaces, our families, our communities, and on the global stage. We see them in individuals who, despite their best intentions, repeatedly make choices that defy common sense.

To tackle the subject of ID10T behavior, we need to first define what it is and what it is not. This book is a guide to understanding the cognitive, behavioral, and emotional aspects of ID10T behavior. It does not aim to label individuals as stupid or dismiss them as unworthy. Instead, it offers insights into the complex factors that contribute to such behavior. These insights are intended to foster empathy and encourage thoughtful responses when confronted with ID10T moments in our own lives or in the lives of others.

The Impact of Stupidity on Individuals and Society

The repercussions of ID10T behavior extend far beyond the immediate moment of folly. These patterns of stupidity affect not only the individuals who exhibit them but also ripple through society, leaving behind a wake of consequences. It is not just about "pointing fingers" or "calling people out." It's about recognizing the broader societal impacts and striving for collective growth and enlightenment.

At the individual level, ID10T moments can lead to personal setbacks, ranging from minor inconveniences to life-altering mistakes. We all have our moments, but understanding why they happen is key to reducing their frequency and impact. By examining these patterns, we empower ourselves to make wiser choices and lead more fulfilling lives.

In our relationships, whether with family, friends, or colleagues, ID10T behavior can strain connections, breed frustration, and lead to misunderstandings. Yet, with knowledge and a measure of patience, we can navigate these challenges more gracefully, enhancing the quality of our relationships and resolving conflicts more effectively.

The societal implications of ID10T behavior are equally profound. The workplace often bears the brunt of these actions, as poor decisions, lack of critical thinking, and questionable judgment can negatively impact productivity and success. Additionally, the political landscape is not immune to the influence of ID10T behavior, with misguided policies and ill-informed decisions having far-reaching consequences on a local, national, and global scale.

Media, as a powerful shaper of public opinion and behavior, plays a pivotal role in either promoting or combatting ID10T behavior. This book will explore the impact of the media's choices in shaping public discourse and provide readers with the tools to navigate the information landscape more effectively.

It is crucial to note that addressing ID10T behavior is not about undermining freedom of expression or stifling diversity of thought. Instead, it's about enhancing individual and collective capacity for critical thinking, empathy, and informed decision-making. We must strive for a society that values intelligence, not as an elitist trait but as a cornerstone of progress and prosperity.

The Purpose of this Book

"ID10T$: Behavioral Patterns of Stupidity" is not a declaration of war against those who make foolish choices. Instead, it is a call for self-reflection and societal improvement. We aim to provide insights and tools to recognize and mitigate ID10T behavior in ourselves and in others. This book is structured to explore the cognitive, emotional, and behavioral aspects of stupidity, while offering practical advice on dealing with these behaviors constructively.

We believe that understanding ID10T behavior is not just a matter of personal growth but a societal imperative. By learning to recognize and address these patterns, we can foster an environment that encourages critical thinking, empathy, and rational decision-making. This book aspires to empower individuals to navigate the complex landscape of human behavior with greater wisdom and compassion.

In the pages that follow, we will explore the origins of ID10T behavior, exploring the cognitive biases that lead to poor decisions and the psychological factors that underpin impulsive actions. We will examine the impact of ID10T behavior in various domains, from the workplace to politics and media. Moreover, we will provide readers with practical strategies and tools for addressing and mitigating ID10T behavior, whether it arises within themselves or others.

It is our hope that this book will exists as a guide for fostering a more intelligent, empathetic, and enlightened society. By recognizing and addressing ID10T behavior, we can collectively work towards a future in which foolish choices and their consequences are less prevalent, and where wisdom and reason are highly valued.

Together, let's begin this journey with open minds and hearts, as we explore the intricate world of ID10T behavior and strive for a better, more enlightened world.

Introduction

In an age where knowledge is at our fingertips, where information flows freely, and where science and reason have propelled us to unprecedented heights, it is perplexing that we find ourselves surrounded by the ubiquitous presence of stupidity. It is a phenomenon that transcends boundaries, impacting people of all backgrounds, races, and socioeconomic statuses. From minor, laughable blunders to devastating, life-altering decisions, stupidity is an omnipresent force, disguising itself in the robes of humor or innocence, infiltrating our lives, and often leaving us dumbfounded or, ironically, shaking our heads.

"ID10T$: Behavioral Patterns of Stupidity" aims to uncover the intricate tapestry of this behavior, delving into the motivations, cognitive biases, and the myriad elements that give birth to such actions. Our purpose is not to mock or condemn but to examine, dissect, and understand. By exploring the cognitive, emotional, and behavioral aspects of stupidity, we can demystify its origins and consequences, paving the way for empathy, growth, and self-improvement.

Defining ID10T Behavior

Before we embark on this journey, it's essential to establish a clear definition of what we mean by "ID10T behavior." This term, derived from "idiot" and commonly used in jest in the digital era, represents a wide spectrum of actions, choices, and patterns that can be classified as moronic, ignorant, or simply foolish. These behaviors extend far beyond momentary lapses of judgment; they encompass recurrent patterns that persist over time.

ID10T behavior can manifest in various forms, including but not limited to:

- **Cognitive Blunders:** These are the lapses in thinking and decision-making that lead to ridiculous or irrational choices. Such blunders can occur in any context, from everyday life decisions to professional settings.

- **Echo Chamber Effect:** When individuals surround themselves with like-minded people, they create a bubble of confirmation bias. This leads to the perpetuation of faulty ideas and ignorance.

- **Dunning-Kruger Effect:** This phenomenon involves individuals overestimating their abilities or knowledge in a particular area. They believe they are more competent than they truly are, often leading to flawed decisions.

- **Impulsivity:** A hallmark of ID10T behavior, impulsivity is characterized by hasty, ill-considered actions with little to no regard for the consequences. It can range from minor impulsive purchases to major life-altering choices.

- **Risk-Taking Behavior:** Some individuals seem addicted to risk, seeking thrills without careful consideration. These actions can lead to a series of ill-advised decisions.

- **Procrastination and Laziness:** The ongoing postponement of tasks or a general lack of motivation and productivity can result in a cycle of missed opportunities and wasted potential.

- **Unintended Consequences:** ID10T behavior often leads to unexpected and undesirable outcomes. These consequences can have a wide-ranging impact, from personal relationships to professional endeavors.

- **The Social Impact of Stupidity:** ID10T behavior doesn't exist in a vacuum; it affects relationships, communication, and the fabric of society. Understanding these social consequences is crucial.

- **ID10T$ in the Workplace:** The impact of stupidity in professional settings can be costly and disruptive. Poor decisions, lack of critical thinking, and impulsivity can hinder productivity and success.

- **Stupidity in Politics:** The influence of ID10T behavior in the political arena is undeniable. Policies and decisions shaped by ignorance can have profound, often far-reaching consequences.

- **ID10T$ and the Media:** Media plays a pivotal role in shaping public opinion and behavior. Recognizing the media's role in either promoting or mitigating ID10T behavior is essential for informed engagement.

To clarify, this exploration is not about pointing fingers, ridiculing, or labeling individuals as "idiots." It is about seeking a deeper understanding of the forces at play in these behaviors. It is about fostering empathy, not only for others but also for oneself. It is about striving for personal growth and collective enlightenment. By recognizing the cognitive biases and psychological factors that contribute to ID10T behavior, we empower ourselves to make wiser choices and lead more fulfilling lives.

The Impact of Stupidity

The impact of ID10T behavior is not confined to the individual making the choices; it reverberates through society, leaving a trail of consequences. Stupidity is not solely about the immediate moment of folly; it's about the ripple effect that extends far beyond the initial action.

On Individuals: ID10T moments can lead to a host of personal setbacks. These range from the minor inconveniences that elicit laughter to more profound, life-altering mistakes that leave us reeling. Understanding why these moments occur is crucial, as it equips us to reduce their frequency and mitigate their impact.

Consider the college student who, due to procrastination and poor decision-making, fails to meet deadlines, jeopardizing their academic future. Or the executive who, enticed by risky financial ventures, gambles away their life savings. In both cases, ID10T behavior has led to detrimental personal consequences.

On Relationships: ID10T behavior is also a significant source of strain in our relationships. Whether within families, among friends, or in the workplace, these behaviors can breed frustration, misunderstandings, and conflicts. Yet, by gaining insight into the nature of ID10T actions, we can navigate these challenges with more grace and patience. We can enhance the quality of our relationships and resolve conflicts more effectively.

Picture the friend who consistently makes impulsive decisions, forcing others to pick up the pieces. Or the family member who procrastinates, leaving a trail of broken promises and strained bonds. Understanding these patterns helps us approach these individuals with empathy and considerate communication.

On the Workplace: ID10T behavior infiltrates professional settings, affecting productivity, decision-making, and overall success. The workplace is not immune to the influence of poor choices, lack of critical thinking, and irrational decisions. This impact can manifest in various ways, from financial losses due to impulsive investments to project delays caused by procrastination.

In the professional sphere, the consequences of ID10T behavior are not limited to individuals alone; they extend to teams, organizations, and even the broader economy. By recognizing these patterns and developing strategies to address them, we can create a more productive and harmonious work environment.

In Politics: The realm of politics is not insulated from the influence of ID10T behavior. Decisions rooted in ignorance or personal bias can have profound effects on the lives of citizens. From poorly crafted policies that fail to address pressing issues to divisive rhetoric that fosters polarization, political ID10T behavior is a widespread concern.

The consequences of such behavior extend to societal division, inefficiency, and economic repercussions. This book will explore the ways in which ID10T behavior infiltrates the political landscape and provide insights into how citizens can engage in informed civic participation.

In the Media: Media, as a dominant force in shaping public opinion, plays a crucial role in either promoting or mitigating ID10T behavior. It can influence the formation of attitudes, beliefs, and behaviors, often on a massive scale. This is not about media bashing or censorship but about media literacy and promoting critical thinking.

Misinformation, sensationalism, and the propagation of biased perspectives can exacerbate ID10T behavior. By understanding these dynamics, readers will be equipped with the tools needed to navigate the media landscape more effectively.

The aim of "ID10T$: Behavioral Patterns of Stupidity" is not to ridicule or belittle those who exhibit these behaviors but to shine a light on the complexity of factors that contribute to them. It seeks to foster empathy, not only for those displaying ID10T behavior but also for ourselves when we stumble into similar traps. This book is a journey of exploration, seeking to unravel the mysteries behind these patterns, and it is a guide for understanding, addressing, and mitigating the impact of ID10T behavior constructively.

Again, throughout the chapters that follow, we will venture into the intricate facets of ID10T behavior, examining the cognitive biases that underpin poor decisions and the psychological factors that give birth to impulsive actions. We will dissect the societal implications of such behavior, from the workplace to politics and the media. We will equip readers with practical strategies and tools to address and mitigate ID10T behavior, whether it arises within themselves or those around them.

The ultimate purpose of this book is to empower individuals to navigate the intricate landscape of human behavior with greater wisdom and compassion. By recognizing and addressing ID10T behavior, we collectively work toward a future in which foolish choices and their consequences are less prevalent, and where intelligence, critical thinking, and empathy are highly valued attributes.

Part I:
Thought Patterns

Chapter 1
The Cognitive Blunders

In our exploration of ID10T behavior, we begin by dissecting one of its fundamental constituents - cognitive blunders. These blunders are not merely instances of forgetfulness or minor oversights; rather, they represent systematic errors in thinking that lead to a series of irrational and often preposterous choices.

Defining Cognitive Blunders

Cognitive blunders, in the context of this discussion, encompass a broad range of faulty thought processes and decision-making mechanisms. They are the missteps that underpin decisions defying logic and reason. Understanding these blunders is a pivotal first step in grasping the essence of ID10T behavior.

Confirmation Bias: One of the most pervasive cognitive blunders, confirmation bias, leads individuals to selectively seek and interpret information that aligns with their existing beliefs and values. This myopic approach to information processing reinforces preconceived notions while neglecting contrary evidence. As a result, it perpetuates ignorance and reinforces ID10T behavior.

Anchoring Bias: Anchoring bias compels individuals to anchor their decisions to the first piece of information they encounter. This initial piece of information then disproportionately influences their choices, despite its potential irrelevance or inaccuracy. This cognitive blunder frequently leads to decisions that deviate from sound judgment.

Hindsight Bias: Hindsight bias, often referred to as the "I-knew-it-all-along" phenomenon, distorts one's perception of past events. Individuals under the influence of this bias tend to believe that they foresaw an event's outcome, even when they had no prior knowledge of it. Such a retrospective self-aggrandizement can foster a misguided sense of foresight.

Availability Heuristic: This cognitive shortcut leads individuals to make decisions based on the readily available information in their memory, rather than thoroughly assessing the true prevalence or probability of an event. The availability heuristic can exaggerate the perceived likelihood of rare or extraordinary occurrences, leading to irrational decisions.

Overconfidence Bias: Overconfidence bias occurs when individuals consistently overestimate their own abilities or knowledge in various domains. This overestimation often results in misguided decisions, as individuals embark on endeavors without a realistic assessment of their competencies.

Sunk Cost Fallacy: The sunk cost fallacy encourages individuals to continue investing in an endeavor or choice, simply because they have already invested time, effort, or resources. This tendency can lead to irrational persistence in failing ventures, fueled by the false belief that past investments warrant future commitment.

The Impact of Cognitive Blunders

The effects of cognitive blunders are manifold, and their repercussions extend well beyond the confines of the momentary lapse in judgment. Recognizing the influence of these blunders is essential for understanding their profound impact on both individuals and society.

On Individuals: Cognitive blunders are not inconsequential errors in thinking; they can significantly affect the lives of individuals. By exploring these effects, we can begin to appreciate the gravity of their influence.

- **Ineffective Decision-Making:** Confirmation bias can lead to poor decision-making. Individuals who disregard contradictory information are more likely to make choices that lead to negative consequences.

- **Missed Opportunities:** Anchoring bias can lead to missed opportunities, as individuals fixate on one piece of information, ignoring potentially more advantageous alternatives.

- **Distorted Self-Perception:** Hindsight bias distorts one's understanding of their own foresight and judgment, often leading to overconfidence and a misguided sense of competence.

- **Risk of Poor Decision-Making:** The availability heuristic can lead to risky decisions, as individuals overestimate the likelihood of certain events based on their memorability.

- **Overcommitment:** Overconfidence bias often results in overcommitment, as individuals take on tasks or challenges for which they are ill-prepared.

- **Continued Investment in Failure:** The sunk cost fallacy can perpetuate investment in failing ventures, contributing to a cycle of loss and disappointment.

On Relationships: Cognitive blunders are not isolated to the individual; they spill over into their relationships with others. The consequences in this domain are multifaceted.

- **Strained Relationships:** Confirmation bias can lead to miscommunication and strained relationships, as individuals dismiss the perspectives and opinions of others.

- **Misunderstandings:** Anchoring bias can cause misunderstandings, as individuals may fail to consider alternate viewpoints or interpretations.

- **Conflict Arising from Misplaced Confidence:** Overconfidence bias can lead to conflict, as individuals assert their competence in situations where they may lack the necessary skills.

- **Interpersonal Friction:** The sunk cost fallacy can result in interpersonal friction, as individuals may insist on pursuing actions that negatively affect those around them.

In the Workplace: The influence of cognitive blunders is pronounced in the professional realm, affecting decision-making, productivity, and overall success.

- **Poor Decision-Making in Business:** Confirmation bias can lead to poor decision-making in business, as individuals dismiss data that contradicts their preconceived notions, often leading to financial losses or missed opportunities.

- **Project Delays:** Anchoring bias can cause project delays, as teams may become fixated on an initial plan, despite its impracticality.

- **Conflict and Inefficiency:** Overconfidence bias can lead to conflict and inefficiency in the workplace, as individuals overestimate their abilities and resist feedback or collaboration.

- **Costly Mistakes:** The sunk cost fallacy can result in costly mistakes, as individuals continue investing in projects that are beyond repair.

In Society: The effects of cognitive blunders extend to society at large, permeating various aspects of public life.

- **Inaccurate Public Discourse:** Confirmation bias can distort public discourse, as individuals gravitate toward sources of information that align with their existing beliefs, often leading to polarization and misinformation.

- **Policy Decisions:** Anchoring bias can influence policy decisions, as political leaders may anchor their positions to their initial stances, even when those stances no longer serve the greater good.

- **Division and Polarization:** Overconfidence bias can fuel division and polarization, as individuals assert their views with unwarranted confidence, dismissing opposing perspectives.

- **Resource Allocation:** The sunk cost fallacy can affect resource allocation, as governments or organizations may persist in funding endeavors with diminishing returns.

Recognizing the prevalence and impact of cognitive blunders is essential for understanding the nature of ID10T behavior. These patterns of thought are not limited to any specific group or demographic; they permeate society and affect individuals from all walks of life. By examining the intricacies of cognitive blunders, we take a significant step toward mitigating the effects of ID10T behavior and fostering a more thoughtful, rational, and informed society.

Ways to Overcome Cognitive Blunders

Understanding cognitive blunders is the first step in mitigating their impact. The next step is to explore strategies for overcoming these systematic errors in thinking. Recognizing and addressing cognitive blunders requires deliberate effort and practice, but the benefits extend to improved decision-making, healthier relationships, and a more rational and empathetic society.

Embrace Critical Thinking: Critical thinking involves questioning assumptions, evaluating evidence, and considering alternative viewpoints. Encouraging critical thinking can counter confirmation bias, anchoring bias, and the availability heuristic, as individuals become more open to diverse perspectives and information.

Develop Self-Awareness: Self-awareness is a cornerstone of combating cognitive blunders. Recognizing one's own cognitive biases and tendencies is the first step toward mitigating their effects. Individuals who are aware of their own overconfidence or susceptibility to confirmation bias are better equipped to counteract these tendencies.

Seek Diverse Perspectives: Expanding one's information sources and engaging with people who hold different viewpoints can help combat confirmation bias and the availability heuristic. Exposure to diverse perspectives challenges preconceived notions and broadens one's understanding.

Encourage Open Dialogue: In relationships and professional settings, encouraging open and honest dialogue can reduce the impact of cognitive blunders. Constructive communication allows for the consideration of different viewpoints and reduces the potential for misunderstandings and conflicts.

Foster a Culture of Learning: In the workplace, organizations can foster a culture of learning and adaptability. This approach allows for the recognition of flawed decisions and the flexibility to change course when necessary, countering the sunk cost fallacy.

Promote Information Literacy: Education in information literacy equips individuals to critically assess information sources, identify biases, and separate fact from fiction. This skill is particularly valuable in the age of abundant information.

Regular Self-Reflection: Periodic self-reflection can help individuals recognize their own cognitive blunders. By reviewing their past decisions and actions, individuals can identify patterns of behavior influenced by cognitive biases.

Feedback and Accountability: Constructive feedback and holding individuals accountable for their decisions are effective tools in addressing cognitive blunders. In professional settings, teams can provide feedback to help colleagues recognize and rectify errors in thinking.

Educational Initiatives: Educational institutions can play a significant role in addressing cognitive blunders by incorporating critical thinking and media literacy into their curricula. These initiatives equip students with the skills needed to navigate the complex information landscape effectively.

Media Literacy Programs: Media organizations can contribute to the reduction of cognitive blunders by promoting media literacy and ethical journalism. This approach helps the public become more discerning consumers of information.

Addressing cognitive blunders is a complex endeavor that necessitates both individual and collective effort. Recognizing and addressing these systematic errors in thinking is an ongoing process that requires self-awareness, the cultivation of critical thinking skills, and a commitment to open dialogue and learning. By taking these steps, individuals and society as a whole can counteract the influence of cognitive blunders.

Chapter 2
The Echo Chamber Effect

As we continue our journey to understand the complexities of ID10T behavior, we turn our focus to the Echo Chamber Effect - a cognitive and social phenomenon that profoundly influences the way we think, the information we encounter, and the decisions we make. It is a concept deeply entwined with the digital age, where the boundless information available at our fingertips paradoxically accelerates our immersion into insular echo chambers.

Defining the Echo Chamber Effect

The Echo Chamber Effect is a term that describes a situation where individuals are surrounded by information, beliefs, or opinions that closely mirror and reinforce their own. It creates a self-perpetuating cycle in which like-minded people interact, validate each other's viewpoints, and often dismiss opposing perspectives. In the realm of ID10T behavior, the Echo Chamber Effect plays a pivotal role, amplifying the flaws in our thinking and contributing to a distorted sense of reality.

Social Media and Digital Platforms: The digital age has given rise to an unprecedented proliferation of social media platforms and online communities. These platforms, while offering remarkable opportunities for connectivity and information-sharing, have also become fertile grounds for the growth of echo chambers.

In this era of curated news feeds, personalized search results, and recommendation algorithms, individuals are often exposed to content that aligns with their preexisting beliefs and preferences. While the intention is to enhance user experience, the consequence is the construction of digital echo chambers.

Selective Exposure: Selective exposure is a behavior that accentuates the Echo Chamber Effect. Individuals tend to seek out and consume information that aligns with their existing beliefs and values. This selective exposure reinforces their existing views and may lead to the dismissal of differing opinions.

Confirmation Bias: At the heart of the Echo Chamber Effect lies confirmation bias. This cognitive bias drives individuals to actively seek information that confirms their existing beliefs while avoiding or discrediting information that contradicts them. This confirmation bias creates a self-reinforcing cycle, as individuals become more entrenched in their own views.

The Consequences
of the Echo Chamber Effect

The consequences of the Echo Chamber Effect are profound and multifaceted. While it may provide a sense of belonging and validation to those within the echo chamber, it also perpetuates ignorance and contributes to ID10T behavior in several ways.

Reinforcement of Ignorance: Echo chambers reinforce individuals' existing beliefs, often without critical examination or consideration of alternative viewpoints. This reinforcement can lead to a skewed understanding of reality, as individuals are sheltered from diverse perspectives and information.

Stifling of Critical Thinking: In an echo chamber, there is little room for critical thinking or skepticism. Individuals within the chamber are unlikely to challenge their own beliefs or engage in healthy debate. This stifling of critical thinking can result in unexamined assumptions and an inability to adapt to new information.

Polarization: The Echo Chamber Effect contributes to societal polarization. When individuals are exposed exclusively to content that supports their own views, they are more likely to view opposing perspectives as extreme or irrational. This polarization can hinder constructive dialogue and compromise.

Disregard for Expertise: The echo chamber often downplays or dismisses expertise and authoritative information that contradicts the prevailing beliefs within the group. This disregard for expertise can lead to misguided decisions and a rejection of science, fact, and evidence.

Emotion Over Rationality: Echo chambers often prioritize emotional responses over rational discourse. When individuals are surrounded by like-minded individuals who validate their emotions, it can become challenging to engage in logical, fact-based discussions.

Amplification of Misinformation: Misinformation that aligns with the beliefs of the echo chamber can spread rapidly within the group. This amplification of misinformation can lead to collective misconceptions and poor decision-making.

Social and Emotional Consequences: The Echo Chamber Effect can have social and emotional consequences, particularly in the context of ID10T behavior. Individuals within echo chambers may experience a false sense of superiority and moral righteousness, leading to condescending or dismissive attitudes toward those outside the group. This can result in social isolation, strained relationships, and confrontations with those who hold opposing views.

Mitigating the Echo Chamber Effect

Recognizing the influence of the Echo Chamber Effect and its role in ID10T behavior is essential for personal and societal growth. While echo chambers are not inherently negative, their potential to perpetuate ignorance and distort reality necessitates mitigation efforts.

Diverse Information Consumption: Actively seeking out diverse sources of information is a powerful strategy to counter the Echo Chamber Effect. Engaging with content and perspectives that challenge one's existing beliefs encourages critical thinking and a more comprehensive understanding of complex issues.

Cross-Pollination of Ideas: Encouraging cross-pollination of ideas is vital in addressing echo chambers. This can be achieved through constructive dialogue and debate with individuals who hold differing viewpoints. Engaging in respectful and empathetic conversations fosters a sense of shared humanity and promotes a deeper understanding of others' perspectives.

Media Literacy: Media literacy programs can equip individuals with the skills to critically assess information sources and recognize bias. These programs are particularly valuable in the digital age, where information is abundant, but misinformation can proliferate unchecked.

Algorithmic Transparency: Digital platforms can contribute to mitigating the Echo Chamber Effect by increasing algorithmic transparency. This involves providing users with clearer information about how content recommendations are generated and the potential for bias in algorithms.

Cultivate a Growth Mindset: Cultivating a growth mindset, which values learning and adaptation, is a powerful antidote to the Echo Chamber Effect. By adopting a growth mindset, individuals are more open to evolving their perspectives and beliefs based on new information.

Encourage Media Diversity: Media organizations and digital platforms can play a role in addressing echo chambers by promoting diverse content and viewpoints. This diversity can enrich the information landscape and encourage a more balanced and inclusive approach to information consumption.

Educational Initiatives: Educational institutions can play a significant role in addressing the Echo Chamber Effect by incorporating critical thinking and empathy into their curricula. These initiatives equip students with the skills needed to engage in diverse perspectives and foster constructive dialogue.

Promote Empathy: Promoting empathy is essential for mitigating the Echo Chamber Effect and addressing ID10T behavior. Empathy encourages individuals to listen actively, understand the perspectives and emotions of others, and engage in compassionate, open-minded dialogue.

Active Bystander Intervention: Encouraging bystanders to intervene when they witness dismissive or confrontational behaviors within echo chambers is another effective strategy. Active bystander intervention promotes a culture of respectful dialogue and discourages behaviors that lead to social isolation and division.

The Echo Chamber Effect is a complex phenomenon that both defines and shapes our information landscape. While it offers a sense of belonging and validation, it also perpetuates ignorance, polarization, and ID10T behavior. Recognizing the Echo Chamber Effect's influence is crucial for personal and societal growth.

Mitigating the Echo Chamber Effect requires a multifaceted approach that encompasses diverse information consumption, cross-pollination of ideas, media literacy, algorithmic transparency, and a cultivation of empathy. Educational initiatives and a commitment to critical thinking play a pivotal role in addressing echo chambers and fostering a more rational, open, and informed society.

As we continue our exploration of thought patterns, we recognize that understanding and mitigating the Echo Chamber Effect is a pivotal step toward reducing ID10T behavior. By embracing diverse perspectives, fostering empathetic dialogue, and promoting critical thinking, we can work toward a future where individuals engage with information and one another in a more thoughtful and enlightened manner.

Chapter 3
The Dunning-Kruger Effect
(Keith Olbermann would appreciate this, I hope)

Continuing on our quest to unravel the complexities of ID10T behavior, we delve into the intricate world of cognitive biases, where the Dunning-Kruger Effect takes center stage. This effect, named after its discoverers, David Dunning and Justin Kruger, is a phenomenon that illuminates how individuals may overestimate their own abilities or knowledge in specific areas, often leading to misguided decisions and behaviors. Understanding the Dunning-Kruger Effect is an essential step in our journey to comprehend the patterns of human thought that contribute to ID10T behavior.

Defining the Dunning-Kruger Effect

The Dunning-Kruger Effect, at its core, is a cognitive bias in which individuals with limited knowledge or expertise in a particular field tend to overestimate their own competence. This overestimation is accompanied by a lack of awareness regarding their lack of expertise. In contrast, individuals who possess genuine expertise tend to underestimate their abilities, assuming that what comes naturally to them is equally intuitive to others.

Unskilled and Unaware: The foundational concept of the Dunning-Kruger Effect centers on the idea that individuals who are less skilled in a particular area are simultaneously less aware of their incompetence. This results in overconfidence and overestimation of their abilities.

Metacognition and Self-Assessment: Metacognition, or the ability to think about one's thinking, plays a crucial role in the Dunning-Kruger Effect. Individuals who lack metacognitive skills are more likely to overestimate their abilities and competence.

The Confidence-Incompetence Loop: The Dunning-Kruger Effect manifests as a confidence-incompetence loop, where individuals with limited knowledge are overly confident in their abilities. Their overconfidence prevents them from recognizing their shortcomings, perpetuating a cycle of misguided decisions and behaviors.

The Consequences of the Dunning-Kruger Effect

The Dunning-Kruger Effect carries significant consequences for individuals, relationships, workplaces, and society as a whole. These consequences stem from the disparity between perceived competence and actual competence.

Ineffective Decision-Making: One of the most immediate consequences of the Dunning-Kruger Effect is ineffective decision-making. Overconfident individuals may make choices and take actions that are based on inaccurate or incomplete information, leading to suboptimal outcomes.

Impaired Problem Solving: The overestimation of one's abilities can impair problem-solving skills. Individuals may rush to solutions without fully understanding the problem or its complexities, often resulting in misguided solutions.

Social and Interpersonal Challenges: The Dunning-Kruger Effect can create social and interpersonal challenges. Overconfident individuals may dismiss the advice and input of others, resulting in strained relationships and conflicts.

Undermining of Expertise: The Dunning-Kruger Effect can undermine genuine expertise. When those with limited knowledge confidently assert their competence, it can lead to the devaluation of true experts and their insights.

Stifling of Learning: Overconfident individuals are less likely to engage in learning and self-improvement. Their belief in their own competence can hinder their willingness to seek new information or to adapt to changing circumstances.

Proliferation of Misinformation: Overconfidence can lead to the spread of misinformation. Individuals may confidently share inaccurate information, believing it to be correct, which can have far-reaching consequences in the age of rapid information dissemination.

Mitigating the Dunning-Kruger Effect

Mitigating the Dunning-Kruger Effect is a multi-faceted endeavor that involves both individual and societal efforts. Recognizing and addressing this cognitive bias is crucial for promoting informed decision-making, fostering humility, and reducing the prevalence of ID10T behavior.

Promote Metacognition: Encouraging metacognition is an essential strategy for mitigating the Dunning-Kruger Effect. Individuals should be taught to reflect on their own thinking, assess their own competence, and recognize their limitations.

Feedback and Evaluation: Providing honest and constructive feedback is a powerful tool for addressing the Dunning-Kruger Effect. Constructive feedback can help individuals become more aware of their competence and shortcomings.

Encourage Lifelong Learning: Emphasizing the value of lifelong learning is crucial. When individuals recognize that knowledge and expertise are dynamic and ever-evolving, they are more likely to engage in self-improvement and ongoing education.

Develop Humility: Cultivating humility is a key aspect of mitigating the Dunning-Kruger Effect. Individuals should be encouraged to acknowledge their limitations, seek assistance when needed, and recognize that true expertise often involves ongoing learning and growth.

Mentorship and Role Models: Mentorship and the presence of role models who embody humility and a commitment to ongoing learning can have a significant impact. These figures can serve as examples of the benefits of recognizing one's limitations and pursuing self-improvement.

Encourage a Growth Mindset: A growth mindset, which embraces challenges and views failure as an opportunity for growth, is a powerful antidote to the Dunning-Kruger Effect. Cultivating a growth mindset fosters a willingness to learn and adapt.

Media Literacy: Promoting media literacy and critical thinking is crucial in addressing the Dunning-Kruger Effect, especially in an era of information overload. Individuals who are media-literate are better equipped to assess the credibility of sources and the accuracy of information.

Supportive and Inclusive Environments: Creating environments that are supportive and inclusive, where individuals feel safe acknowledging their limitations and seeking help, is essential. Such environments reduce the fear of appearing incompetent and promote a culture of learning.

Educational Initiatives: Educational institutions play a pivotal role in mitigating the Dunning-Kruger Effect by incorporating metacognitive skills, humility, and self-assessment into their curricula. These initiatives equip students with the skills needed to navigate the complexities of competence and knowledge.

The Dunning-Kruger Effect is a cognitive bias that affects individuals across various domains, from personal decision-making to professional interactions and societal discourse.

Mitigating the Dunning-Kruger Effect requires a commitment to promoting metacognition, humility, lifelong learning, feedback, and a growth mindset. These strategies empower individuals to acknowledge their limitations, embrace ongoing education, and make more informed decisions.

Part II
Action Patterns

Chapter 4
Impulsivity and
Its Consequences

As we transition from the realm of thought patterns into the realm of action patterns in our exploration of ID10T behavior, we encounter a behavioral trait that often serves as a catalyst for foolish decisions and reckless actions - impulsivity. Impulsivity is a characteristic marked by hasty decision-making, a disregard for consequences, and a failure to consider the long-term impact of one's actions. Let's get into the nature of impulsivity, its underlying factors, and the profound consequences it can have on individuals and society.

Defining Impulsivity

Impulsivity is a behavioral trait characterized by a lack of forethought or consideration of the consequences of one's actions. Individuals who exhibit impulsivity tend to act without sufficient reflection, often driven by immediate desires, emotions, or external stimuli. Impulsivity can manifest in various ways, from impulsive purchases to rash decisions with far-reaching consequences.

Factors Underlying Impulsivity

The origins of impulsivity are multifaceted and may be influenced by a combination of genetic, neurological, and environmental factors. Understanding these underlying factors can shed light on why some individuals are more prone to impulsivity than others.

Neurological Factors: Impulsivity is associated with the functioning of specific regions of the brain, particularly the prefrontal cortex. This area of the brain is responsible for executive functions such as planning, decision-making, and impulse control. Differences in the structure or function of the prefrontal cortex can contribute to impulsivity.

Genetic Predisposition: Genetic factors play a role in impulsivity. Some individuals may have a genetic predisposition to impulsivity, which can be further influenced by the presence of specific gene variants. Genetic research has identified links between impulsivity and certain genes.

Environmental Influences: Environmental factors, particularly early-life experiences, can also contribute to impulsivity. Childhood trauma, neglect, or exposure to stressors can impact the development of self-regulation and impulse control.

Psychological Traits: Certain psychological traits, such as sensation-seeking and low conscientiousness, are associated with impulsivity. Individuals who seek novelty, excitement, and thrills are more likely to engage in impulsive behavior.

Consequences of Impulsivity

Impulsivity is not merely a personality trait; it carries significant consequences for individuals and society as a whole. These consequences extend beyond the immediate aftermath of impulsive actions and can have far-reaching effects.

- **Personal Consequences:** Impulsivity can result in a range of personal consequences for individuals.

- **Financial Troubles:** Impulsive spending and financial decisions can lead to debt and financial instability.

- **Health Risks:** Impulsive behaviors can put one's health at risk, such as engaging in risky sexual behavior or substance abuse.

- **Strained Relationships:** Impulsivity in

communication or emotional reactions can lead to strained relationships with friends, family, and colleagues.

- **Legal Issues:** Impulsive actions can result in legal troubles, from minor offenses to more serious crimes.

- **Missed Opportunities:** Impulsivity can lead to missed opportunities in education, career advancement, and personal growth.

Workplace Consequences: Impulsivity in the workplace can have significant implications.

- **Decreased Productivity:** Impulsive actions at work can lead to decreased productivity and poor time management.

- **Conflict with Colleagues:** Impulsivity in communication or decision-making can result in conflicts with colleagues.

- **Career Stagnation:** Impulsivity may hinder career progression by leading to poorly considered decisions or actions that damage one's professional reputation.

- **Financial Loss for Employers:** Impulsivity can result in financial losses for employers when employees make costly mistakes or engage in embezzlement.

Social and Societal Consequences: Impulsivity can affect society on a broader scale.

- **Traffic Accidents:** Impulsivity, particularly in the context of road rage or reckless driving, can lead to traffic accidents with severe consequences.

- **Public Safety:** Impulsive actions can pose risks to public safety, such as acts of violence or vandalism.

- **Criminal Activity:** Impulsivity can contribute to criminal activity, from impulsive theft to acts of violence.

- **Healthcare Costs:** Impulsivity-related health issues, such as accidents or injuries, can result in increased healthcare costs for society.

Impulsivity in the Age of Technology

In the digital age, impulsivity takes on new dimensions. The rapid pace of online interactions, the constant stream of information, and the allure of instant gratification can exacerbate impulsive behaviors.

Online Shopping: Impulsive online shopping, driven by one-click purchasing and enticing deals, has become a common issue. Individuals may make impulsive purchases they later regret.

Social Media: Impulsive posting on social media, from sharing emotional rants to engaging in online conflicts, can have lasting consequences for one's personal and professional life.

Cyberbullying: Impulsive cyberbullying and online harassment can lead to psychological harm and legal repercussions.

Cybersecurity Risks: Impulsivity can put individuals at risk of cybersecurity breaches, such as falling for phishing scams or sharing sensitive information online.

Mitigating Impulsivity and Its Consequences

Addressing impulsivity and its consequences is a complex endeavor that involves both individual and collective efforts. Mitigating impulsivity requires developing self-regulation, self-awareness, and a proactive approach to decision-making.

Cultivate Self-Awareness: Self-awareness is the foundation of addressing impulsivity. Individuals who recognize their own impulsive tendencies are better equipped to control and manage them.

Mindfulness Practices: Mindfulness practices, such as meditation and deep breathing exercises, can help individuals become more attuned to their thoughts and emotions, reducing the likelihood of impulsive reactions.

Emotion Regulation: Learning to regulate one's emotions is essential for addressing impulsivity. Individuals can benefit from strategies that help them manage strong emotions without impulsive actions.

Cognitive-Behavioral Therapy (CBT): CBT is an evidence-based approach that can be effective in addressing impulsivity. This therapy helps individuals identify thought patterns that lead to impulsive behaviors and develop healthier coping strategies.

Delayed Gratification: Practicing delayed gratification

involves intentionally postponing immediate desires in favor of long-term goals. This approach can reduce impulsivity in decision-making.

Decision-Making Strategies: Individuals can benefit from adopting decision-making strategies that involve weighing the pros and cons, considering consequences, and seeking input from others.

Setting Boundaries: Establishing personal boundaries, particularly in online activities, can help individuals manage impulsivity. This includes limiting time spent on social media, setting rules for online shopping, and recognizing signs of impulsivity.

Peer and Social Support: Peer and social support can play a pivotal role in addressing impulsivity. Friends and family can offer guidance, encouragement, and accountability in managing impulsive behaviors.

Media Literacy: Media literacy programs can help individuals become more discerning consumers of online content, reducing impulsive sharing or engagement in online conflicts.

Legal and Policy Measures: Societal efforts can include legal and policy measures that deter impulsivity-related issues, such as cyberbullying or reckless online behavior.

Impulsivity is a behavioral trait that significantly influences decision-making and actions, often leading to unintended consequences for individuals and society.

Mitigating impulsivity involves the cultivation of self-awareness, the practice of mindfulness, emotion regulation, cognitive-behavioral therapy, and decision-making strategies. By addressing impulsivity at both the individual and societal levels, we can foster a more thoughtful, reflective, and self-regulated society, ultimately reducing the prevalence of ID10T behavior.

Chapter 5
Risk-Taking Behavior

Now we transition from the realm of impulsivity to a closely related behavioral trait that often amplifies the consequences of foolish decisions and actions - risk-taking behavior. Risk-taking, when unchecked and devoid of thoughtful consideration, can lead individuals down perilous paths, causing harm to themselves and society at large. This chapter examines the nature of risk-taking behavior, the psychological mechanisms that underpin it, and the far-reaching consequences it can have.

Defining Risk-Taking Behavior

Risk-taking behavior is a trait characterized by a willingness to engage in actions or decisions that carry a significant degree of uncertainty and the potential for negative consequences. It involves venturing into the unknown or making choices with potentially harmful outcomes, often driven by a desire for excitement, novelty, or the pursuit of rewards.

Psychological Underpinnings of Risk-Taking Behavior

Risk-taking behavior is rooted in several psychological mechanisms and cognitive processes that influence individuals' choices and actions. Understanding these mechanisms is crucial for comprehending the nature of risk-taking and its impact.

Reward-Seeking: One of the primary drivers of risk-taking behavior is the pursuit of rewards. Individuals who engage in risk-taking often do so with the anticipation of positive outcomes, such as financial gain, social approval, or exhilaration.

Sensation-Seeking: Sensation-seeking is a psychological trait associated with a desire for novel, exciting, and stimulating experiences. Individuals with high levels of sensation-seeking are more inclined to engage in risky behaviors to satisfy their need for excitement.

Impaired Decision-Making: Impaired decision-making can lead to risk-taking behavior. Factors such as impulsivity or cognitive biases may cloud individuals' judgment, causing them to underestimate the potential negative consequences of their actions.

Emotional States: Emotional states, particularly those associated with stress, anxiety, or heightened arousal, can drive individuals to take risks. These emotions can create a sense of urgency or a desire to escape discomfort, leading to impulsive, risk-taking decisions.

Social and Peer Influence: Social and peer influence can play a significant role in risk-taking behavior. Individuals may take risks to conform to group norms or to seek approval and validation from their peers.

The Consequences
of Risk-Taking Behavior

The consequences of risk-taking behavior are multifaceted and extend beyond the immediate outcomes of a risky decision or action. These consequences can impact individuals, their relationships, the workplace, and society as a whole.

Personal Consequences: Risk-taking behavior often results in personal consequences for individuals.

- **Physical Injury**: Engaging in reckless activities or dangerous stunts can lead to physical injury, ranging from minor accidents to life-threatening harm.

- **Financial Loss:** Risk-taking in financial matters, such as high-stakes gambling or speculative investments, can result in significant financial losses.

- **Psychological Stress:** Risk-taking decisions, especially when they lead to adverse outcomes, can result in psychological stress, anxiety, and emotional turmoil.

- **Health Risks:** Engaging in risky behaviors, such as substance abuse or unprotected sexual activity, can put one's health at risk, leading to long-term health problems.

- **Legal Consequences:** Risk-taking actions that violate laws or regulations can result in legal consequences, including fines, imprisonment, or criminal records.

Interpersonal Consequences: Risk-taking behavior can strain interpersonal relationships and lead to conflicts.

- **Family Discord:** Risk-taking decisions may create tension within families, as loved ones may be concerned about the individual's safety or well-being.

- **Friendship Strain:** Friends may experience strain in their relationships with individuals who consistently engage in risky behavior, as they may be reluctant to participate or disapprove of such actions.

- **Colleague Conflicts:** Risk-taking behavior in the workplace can lead to conflicts with colleagues, especially when decisions impact team projects or organizational goals.

- **Deterioration of Relationships:** Repeated risk-taking behavior can lead to the deterioration of personal and professional relationships, as individuals may become alienated or ostracized by those who disapprove of their actions.

Workplace Consequences: In the workplace, risk-taking behavior can have significant implications.

- **Decreased Productivity:** Risk-taking decisions, especially when they result in adverse consequences, can lead to decreased productivity and job performance.

- **Safety Concerns:** Risk-taking behavior may pose safety concerns for the workplace, particularly in high-risk industries where safety protocols are paramount.

- **Career Implications:** Engaging in reckless actions or decisions can have long-term career implications, such as job loss or difficulty finding future employment.

- **Reputation Damage:** Risk-taking behavior in a professional context can lead to damage to one's professional reputation, which may impact future career opportunities.

Societal Consequences: On a broader societal scale, risk-taking behavior can have significant repercussions.

- **Public Health Costs:** High-risk behaviors, such as substance abuse or reckless driving, contribute to public health costs, including medical treatment and rehabilitation expenses.

- **Law Enforcement Resources:** Risk-taking actions that result in legal consequences require the allocation of law enforcement resources and can burden the legal system.

- **Resource Allocation:** Engaging in risky financial or business decisions can impact resource allocation, as individuals or organizations may require financial support or intervention.

Mitigating Risk-Taking Behavior

Mitigating risk-taking behavior is a complex undertaking that necessitates a combination of individual awareness, self-regulation, education, and supportive societal measures.

Promote Risk Awareness: Individuals can benefit from enhancing their awareness of potential risks and consequences. Understanding the potential harms of risky actions can serve as a deterrent.

Emotional Regulation: Emotion regulation skills are essential for managing impulsive risk-taking behavior. Individuals can benefit from strategies that help them control emotional impulses and make decisions with a clear mind.

Educational Initiatives: Educational institutions can play a pivotal role in promoting risk awareness and responsible decision-making. Incorporating risk education into curricula can equip students with the knowledge and skills needed to make informed choices.

Peer and Social Support: Peer and social support systems can help individuals resist the pressures of engaging in risky behavior. Friends and family can provide guidance and encouragement.

Counseling and Therapy: When risk-taking behavior is driven by underlying psychological issues, counseling and therapy can be highly effective in addressing these root causes and developing healthier coping strategies.

Responsible Marketing: Companies and industries can play a role in responsible marketing and advertising. Ensuring that promotional materials do not glorify or encourage risky behavior is vital.

Safety Regulations: In high-risk industries, strict safety regulations and protocols can help minimize the potential for accidents and harm caused by risk-taking behavior.

Legal Deterrents: Legal measures can act as a deterrent to risk-taking behavior by imposing consequences for illegal or reckless actions. These measures include fines, penalties, and imprisonment.

Risk-taking behavior is a trait that can lead individuals to make decisions and take actions with the potential for adverse consequences.

Mitigating risk-taking behavior requires promoting risk awareness, emotional regulation, education, peer and social support, counseling, responsible marketing, safety regulations, and legal deterrents. By fostering a more informed, responsible, and safety-conscious society, we can reduce the prevalence of risk-taking behavior and the associated consequences.

Chapter 6
Procrastination and Laziness

As we continue, we confront a set of tendencies that hinder productivity, sabotage personal growth, and breed a culture of inaction - procrastination and laziness. These action patterns, driven by a desire to delay tasks, avoid effort, and seek momentary comfort, can lead to poor decision-making and adverse consequences. This chapter delves into the nature of procrastination and laziness, the underlying factors that fuel them, and the profound implications they have on individuals and society.

Defining Procrastination and Laziness

Procrastination is a behavior marked by the deliberate delay of tasks or actions, often leading to less-than-optimal outcomes and increased stress. It involves postponing activities that require effort, mental focus, or may lead to discomfort.

Laziness, on the other hand, is a state of inactivity or a disinclination to expend effort. It implies a reluctance to engage in productive activities, instead favoring idleness or activities that require minimal energy or thought.

Psychological Mechanisms Underlying Procrastination and Laziness

The roots of procrastination and laziness lie in several psychological mechanisms that influence individuals' actions and decision-making processes.

Instant Gratification: The desire for immediate pleasure or comfort can lead to procrastination and laziness, as individuals prioritize momentary enjoyment over long-term rewards.

Avoidance of Discomfort: Procrastination often arises from a desire to avoid discomfort or negative emotions associated with a task. Individuals may delay actions to escape feelings of stress, anxiety, or boredom.

Low Self-Efficacy: Low self-efficacy, or the belief in one's ability to perform a task successfully, can contribute to procrastination and laziness. Individuals who doubt their competence may avoid tasks to prevent failure.

Perfectionism: Perfectionism can lead to procrastination, as individuals set unrealistically high standards for their work. Fearing they cannot meet these standards, they may delay tasks indefinitely.

Decisional Procrastination: Decisional procrastination pertains to the avoidance of making decisions, which can lead to a state of inaction. The fear of making the wrong choice or facing the consequences of a decision can result in persistent indecision.

The Consequences
of Procrastination and Laziness

Procrastination and laziness bring a host of consequences that affect individuals, their relationships, their work, and society at large.

Personal Consequences: The personal ramifications of procrastination and laziness include:

- **Missed Opportunities:** Procrastination can lead to missed opportunities, both professionally and personally, as individuals delay actions that could have advanced their careers or enriched their lives.

- **Decreased Productivity:** Laziness and

procrastination result in decreased productivity, as tasks are delayed or left unfinished.

- **Increased Stress:** Procrastination can cause elevated stress levels as individuals scramble to complete tasks at the last minute, often resulting in lower-quality work.

- **Health Implications:** Procrastination and laziness can have health implications, such as sedentary lifestyles and neglected self-care routines.

Financial Consequences: Delaying financial tasks, such as paying bills or managing investments, can lead to financial penalties or missed opportunities for savings and investment.

Relationship Consequences: Procrastination and laziness can strain relationships in several ways:

- **Unmet Obligations:** When individuals fail to fulfill their commitments, it can lead to disappointment and frustration among friends, family, and colleagues.

- **Increased Dependence:** Procrastination and laziness may lead to increased dependence on others, as individuals rely on them to compensate for their inaction.

- **Communication Issues:** Delaying important conversations or addressing issues can create communication problems within relationships.

- **Loss of Trust:** Repeated instances of procrastination or laziness can erode trust in relationships, leading to doubts about one's reliability.

Workplace Consequences: In the workplace, the impact of procrastination and laziness extends to:

- **Missed Deadlines:** Procrastination often results in missed project deadlines, causing delays and potentially harming the organization.

- **Reduced Quality:** Laziness and procrastination can lead to lower-quality work, affecting the organization's reputation and success.

- **Decline in Motivation:** A workplace culture that tolerates procrastination and laziness can foster a decline in motivation and productivity among employees.

- **Conflict with Colleagues:** Procrastination can result in conflicts with colleagues who must pick up the slack due to delayed work.

- **Career Stagnation:** Consistent procrastination and laziness can hinder career progression, as individuals fail to meet performance expectations.

Societal Consequences: Procrastination and laziness contribute to societal challenges:

- **Economic Impact:** Inefficiencies resulting from procrastination and laziness can have a negative economic impact on a national scale.

- **Resource Waste:** When individuals procrastinate or engage in lazy behaviors, resources such as time, energy, and materials are often wasted.

- **Healthcare Costs:** Sedentary lifestyles associated with laziness contribute to rising healthcare costs related to obesity, heart disease, and other health issues.

- **Educational Implications:** Procrastination can hinder educational progress, leading to lower academic achievement and reduced educational outcomes.

Mitigating Procrastination and Laziness

Addressing procrastination and laziness requires a multifaceted approach that encompasses individual awareness, self-regulation, educational initiatives, and supportive societal measures.

Self-Awareness: Developing self-awareness of one's procrastination and laziness tendencies is the first step in addressing these behaviors. Individuals should recognize their patterns of inaction and the reasons behind them.

Goal Setting: Setting clear and achievable goals is a powerful strategy for combating procrastination and laziness. Goals provide a sense of purpose and direction, motivating individuals to take action.

Time Management: Effective time management strategies can help individuals organize their tasks, allocate time appropriately, and reduce procrastination.

Motivation Enhancement: Enhancing motivation involves identifying and leveraging intrinsic and extrinsic motivators to drive action. Individuals can find purpose and inspiration in their goals.

Self-Discipline: Cultivating self-discipline is vital for overcoming procrastination and laziness. This involves making a conscious effort to stick to a plan and resist the urge to delay tasks.

Cognitive-Behavioral Therapy (CBT): CBT is a therapeutic approach that can be effective in addressing procrastination and laziness. It helps individuals recognize unhelpful thought patterns and develop healthier beliefs and behaviors.

Peer and Social Support: Peer and social support systems can help individuals stay accountable and motivated to overcome procrastination and laziness.

Education and Awareness: Educational initiatives that promote awareness of procrastination and provide tools and strategies to address it can be highly effective in mitigating these behaviors.

Workplace Culture: Fostering a workplace culture that values productivity, time management, and clear expectations can reduce procrastination and laziness.

Legal and Policy Measures: In some cases, legal and policy measures may be necessary to address procrastination and laziness in areas such as education or work.

Procrastination and laziness are action patterns that hinder personal growth, strain relationships, and have broader societal implications. Understanding the psychological mechanisms behind these behaviors and their consequences is essential in addressing these behaviors.

Mitigating procrastination and laziness requires self-awareness, goal setting, time management, motivation enhancement, self-discipline, cognitive-behavioral therapy, peer and social support, education, workplace culture changes, and, in some cases, legal and policy measures. By fostering a culture of productivity, responsibility, and action, we can reduce the prevalence of procrastination and laziness, moving closer to a society that is more thoughtful, motivated, and enlightened.

Part III
Deed Patterns

Chapter 7
Unintended Consequences

In our exploration of ID10T behavior, we journey deeper into the realm of action patterns, seeking to understand a phenomenon that often wreaks havoc on the best-laid plans and decisions - unintended consequences. These are the unexpected, adverse outcomes that result from actions or decisions made with good intentions, ignorance, or neglect. In this chapter, we unravel the nature of unintended consequences, the factors that contribute to them, and the profound impact they can have on individuals and society.

Defining Unintended Consequences

Unintended consequences, often referred to as "side effects" or "ripple effects," are outcomes that are not anticipated or intended when an action or decision is made. They can manifest in a variety of ways, from minor inconveniences to major disruptions, and may occur in personal, professional, or societal contexts.

Factors Contributing to Unintended Consequences

Unintended consequences can be traced to several contributing factors that influence the outcomes of actions and decisions.

Complexity of Systems: In complex systems, such as economies, organizations, or ecosystems, multiple interrelated variables make it challenging to predict all potential outcomes of an action.

Limited Knowledge: Unintended consequences often result from a lack of comprehensive knowledge about the circumstances, potential impacts, or interactions involved in a decision.

Unforeseen Interactions: Actions and decisions may set off a chain of unforeseen interactions and reactions, leading to outcomes that were not initially apparent.

Short-Term Focus: A short-term focus on immediate gains can blind individuals to the long-term, indirect consequences of their actions.

Moral Hazard: Moral hazard refers to the tendency for individuals to take more risks when they believe they will not bear the full consequences of their actions, as seen in certain financial, insurance, or environmental contexts.

The Consequences of Unintended Consequences

Unintended consequences can have wide-ranging and profound implications at personal, organizational, and societal levels.

Personal Consequences: Individuals may experience the following personal ramifications:

- **Stress and Anxiety:** Unintended consequences can lead to stress and anxiety, as individuals grapple with the unforeseen challenges or difficulties they now face.

- **Financial Loss:** Financial decisions with unintended consequences can result in unexpected expenses, debt, or lost opportunities for savings or investment.

- **Health Impact:** Actions with unintended health consequences may lead to physical or psychological health issues, demanding medical attention or lifestyle changes.

- **Relationship Strain:** Unintended consequences can strain personal relationships, as individuals must address unexpected challenges or disruptions.

- **Emotional Toll:** Coping with unintended consequences can take an emotional toll, resulting in frustration, disappointment, or regret.

Workplace Consequences: In the workplace, unintended consequences can lead to:

- **Operational Disruptions:** Unforeseen disruptions may occur due to unintended consequences, affecting productivity and workflow.

- **Reputation Damage:** Adverse outcomes can tarnish an organization's reputation, eroding trust and causing financial losses.

- **Legal Issues:** Unintended consequences may result in legal complications or liabilities, requiring legal action or settlements.

- **Employee Morale:** Workplace morale may decline due to the stress and uncertainty caused by unintended consequences.

- **Financial Impact:** Economic losses may accrue as a result of unexpected costs or reductions in revenue.

Societal Consequences: Unintended consequences can

have a significant societal impact:

- **Economic Ramifications:** Adverse outcomes in economic policies, financial decisions, or market behavior can lead to economic crises or recessions.

- **Environmental Impact:** Unintended consequences of environmental decisions can result in pollution, resource depletion, or ecosystem disruptions.

- **Healthcare Challenges:** Unintended consequences in healthcare policy or medical practice can strain healthcare systems, hinder patient care, or lead to public health issues.

- **Legal and Policy Reforms:** Unintended consequences may necessitate legal or policy reforms to address the issues that arise.

Mitigating Unintended Consequences

Addressing unintended consequences is a complex task that requires vigilance, comprehensive knowledge, long-term perspective, and a proactive approach to decision-making.

Comprehensive Knowledge: Decision-makers should strive to gather comprehensive knowledge about the context and potential ramifications of their actions.

Risk Assessment: Conducting risk assessments can help individuals and organizations identify potential unintended consequences before they occur.

Long-Term Perspective: Considering the long-term implications of actions and decisions can prevent individuals from being shortsighted and ignoring potential future side effects.

Scenario Planning: Scenario planning involves envisioning different potential outcomes of actions and decisions, which can help in anticipating and addressing unintended consequences.

Safeguards and Contingencies: Building safeguards and contingency plans into actions and decisions can help mitigate the impact of unintended consequences if they do occur.

Adaptive Strategies: When unintended consequences do occur, the ability to adapt and respond effectively is crucial. This may involve making changes, seeking solutions, or mitigating the damage.

Transparency and Accountability: Organizations and institutions should promote transparency and accountability in decision-making processes, enabling stakeholders to understand potential consequences and hold decision-makers responsible.

Legal and Ethical Frameworks: Legal and ethical frameworks should be in place to address unintended consequences, offering guidelines for appropriate responses and resolutions.

Public Awareness and Education: Public awareness and education campaigns can help individuals and communities understand the potential consequences of their actions and make informed choices.

Unintended consequences are a common and pervasive element of actions and decisions. Mitigating unintended consequences involves comprehensive knowledge, risk assessment, a long-term perspective, scenario planning, safeguards, adaptive strategies, transparency, legal and ethical frameworks, and public awareness and education. By fostering a culture of responsible decision-making and proactive risk management, we can reduce the prevalence of unintended consequences and work toward a society that is more thoughtful, informed, and enlightened.

Chapter 8
The Social Impact
of Stupidity

We have now arrived at a junction where the personal gives way to the societal, where the actions of individuals collectively give birth to a phenomenon that has profound implications for our communities - the social impact of stupidity. This chapter delves into the nature of the social impact of stupidity, its underlying factors, and the ways in which it shapes our collective experiences.

Defining the Social Impact of Stupidity

The social impact of stupidity is the collective consequence of foolish, ill-considered, or uninformed actions within a society. It encompasses a wide range of behaviors that hinder progress, create divisions, and strain social cohesion. These behaviors can manifest in various ways, from the adoption of irrational beliefs to the spread of misinformation, and from participation in reckless actions to the neglect of long-term consequences.

Factors Underlying
the Social Impact of Stupidity

Understanding the social impact of stupidity requires a closer look at the factors that contribute to this phenomenon on a collective level:

Cognitive Biases: Cognitive biases are ingrained tendencies that affect how individuals perceive and interpret information. These biases can lead people to make irrational decisions or hold false beliefs.

Groupthink: Groupthink occurs when a desire for consensus within a group results in conformity and the suppression of dissenting opinions, often leading to ill-advised decisions.

Confirmation Bias: Confirmation bias is the tendency to

seek and interpret information in ways that confirm preexisting beliefs while ignoring contradictory evidence, fostering ignorance and reinforcing foolish notions.

Echo Chambers: Echo chambers are closed, self-reinforcing environments where individuals interact only with like-minded people, leading to the amplification of irrational beliefs and the rejection of opposing viewpoints.

Herding Behavior: Herding behavior is the tendency of individuals to follow the actions and decisions of the majority, even when these actions are unwise, resulting in the propagation of stupidity.

The Social Impact of Stupidity

The social impact of stupidity has far-reaching implications, affecting multiple facets of society:

Erosion of Trust: The spread of irrational beliefs and misinformation erodes trust within society, creating divisions and undermining collective decision-making.

Economic Consequences: Foolish economic decisions, driven by ill-informed beliefs or short-term thinking, can lead to financial crises, market volatility, and economic inequality.

Healthcare Challenges: Misguided health-related decisions, such as refusal of vaccinations or adherence to unproven treatments, can lead to public health issues and strain healthcare systems.

Environmental Degradation: Irresponsible environmental choices, like disregarding conservation efforts or neglecting the consequences of pollution, result in ecological damage and loss of natural resources.

Political Dysfunction: The social impact of stupidity can manifest in the form of misguided political decisions, divisiveness, and gridlock, hindering the enactment of effective policies and solutions.

Loss of Innovation: A culture of irrationality and resistance to new ideas can stifle innovation and limit societal progress.

Crisis Response: In times of crisis, such as natural disasters or public health emergencies, foolish decisions can lead to inefficient response efforts and greater suffering.

Mitigating the Social Impact of Stupidity

Addressing the social impact of stupidity is a multifaceted endeavor that necessitates a commitment to education, critical thinking, awareness, and responsible leadership.

Promote Critical Thinking: Fostering critical thinking skills within society is crucial for reducing the social impact of stupidity. Critical thinking enables individuals to evaluate information, challenge irrational beliefs, and make informed decisions.

Media Literacy: Promoting media literacy helps individuals distinguish between reliable information and misinformation. This reduces the impact of false narratives and irrational beliefs.

Educational Initiatives: Educational institutions play a vital role in equipping individuals with the knowledge and skills needed to think critically and make informed decisions.

Diversity of Perspectives: Encouraging diversity of

perspectives and open dialogue can help break down echo chambers and reduce groupthink, enabling a more well-rounded understanding of issues.

Responsible Leadership: Leaders in various fields, including politics, business, and education, should model responsible decision-making and prioritize evidence-based approaches.

Fact-Checking and Accountability: Fact-checking initiatives and accountability measures can help identify and rectify misinformation, reducing the influence of irrational beliefs.

Promote Rational Public Discourse: Public discourse should be characterized by rational and respectful exchange of ideas, rather than ad hominem attacks or emotional appeals.

Crisis Preparedness: Society should prioritize crisis preparedness and response strategies that are evidence-based, enabling effective responses in times of crisis.

The social impact of stupidity is a complex and pervasive phenomenon that affects all levels of society, from individuals to communities and nations.

Mitigating the social impact of stupidity involves promoting critical thinking, media literacy, educational initiatives, diversity of perspectives, responsible leadership, fact-checking, accountability, and rational public discourse. By fostering a culture of rationality, evidence-based decision-making, and open dialogue, we can work towards a society that is more informed, cohesive, and enlightened.

Chapter 9
The Road to Self-Destruction

In our continued exploration, we venture into a territory where personal choices and actions intertwine with the potential for dire consequences – the road to self-destruction. This chapter delves into the nature of self-destructive behavior, the psychological factors that underlie it, and the profound implications it has on individuals and society as a whole.

Defining Self-Destructive Behavior

Self-destructive behavior is characterized by actions or decisions that jeopardize an individual's physical, psychological, or social well-being. It often involves choices that knowingly lead to harm, despite the availability of alternative, healthier options. Self-destructive behavior can manifest in various forms, such as substance abuse, self-harm, risky sexual behavior, and excessive procrastination.

Psychological Underpinnings of Self-Destructive Behavior

Understanding self-destructive behavior requires an examination of the psychological factors and cognitive processes that drive individuals to make choices detrimental to their own well-being.

Emotional Dysregulation: Self-destructive behavior often stems from difficulties in regulating emotions. Individuals may resort to self-destructive actions as a way to cope with intense emotions, such as anger, sadness, or anxiety.

Low Self-Esteem: A negative self-perception can lead to self-destructive behavior, as individuals may engage in actions that confirm their belief in their own unworthiness.

Coping Mechanisms: Self-destructive actions can serve as coping mechanisms to numb emotional pain, escape distressing situations, or gain a temporary sense of relief.

Impulsivity: Impulsivity, characterized by hasty and thoughtless decision-making, can result in self-destructive actions that individuals later regret.

Addictive Behavior: Self-destructive behavior often includes addictions, where individuals become dependent on substances or behaviors that are harmful but temporarily pleasurable.

The Consequences of Self-Destructive Behavior

Self-destructive behavior carries profound and often long-lasting consequences for individuals, their relationships, their careers, and society as a whole.

Personal Consequences: On a personal level, individuals may experience the following ramifications of self-destructive behavior:

- **Physical Harm:** Actions such as substance abuse, self-harm, or risky sexual behavior can lead to physical injuries or health problems.

- **Psychological Distress:** Self-destructive behavior is often accompanied by psychological distress, including depression, anxiety, or self-loathing.

- **Financial Hardship:** Engaging in addictive behaviors can result in financial hardship as individuals prioritize their addiction over essential expenses.

- **Social Isolation:** Self-destructive actions may lead to social isolation, as individuals withdraw from friends and family or alienate loved ones.

Legal Consequences: Some self-destructive behaviors, such as criminal activities or substance abuse, may have legal repercussions, including fines or imprisonment.

Relationship Consequences: Self-destructive behavior can strain personal relationships in the following ways:

- **Trust Erosion:** Repeated instances of self-destructive behavior can erode trust in relationships, causing loved ones to doubt the individual's reliability.

- **Emotional Toll:** Loved ones may experience emotional distress when witnessing self-destructive actions and their consequences.

- **Relationship Breakdown:** In some cases, self-destructive behavior can lead to the breakdown of relationships, as loved ones may be unable to continue supporting the individual's actions.

Workplace Consequences: In the workplace, self-destructive behavior can lead to:

- **Decreased Productivity:** Self-destructive actions often result in decreased productivity and job performance.

- **Conflict with Colleagues:** Co-workers

may experience conflict with individuals engaging in self-destructive behavior, especially when their actions impact team projects or organizational goals.

- **Career Implications:** Consistent self-destructive behavior can hinder career progression, as individuals fail to meet performance expectations.

- **Reputation Damage:** Self-destructive behavior in a professional context can lead to damage to one's professional reputation, which may impact future career opportunities.

Societal Consequences: On a broader societal scale, self-destructive behavior can have significant repercussions:

- **Public Health Costs:** High-risk behaviors, such as substance abuse or reckless driving, contribute to public health costs, including medical treatment and rehabilitation expenses.

- **Law Enforcement Resources:** Self-destructive actions that result in legal consequences require the allocation of law enforcement resources and can burden the legal system.

- **Resource Allocation:** Engaging in risky financial or business decisions can impact resource allocation, as individuals or organizations may require financial support or intervention.

Mitigating Self-Destructive Behavior

Addressing self-destructive behavior involves a multifaceted approach encompassing individual awareness, self-regulation, counseling and therapy, and societal support systems.

Self-Awareness: Developing self-awareness of one's self-destructive tendencies is the first step in addressing this behavior. Individuals should recognize their patterns of self-harm and the reasons behind them.

Emotion Regulation: Emotion regulation skills are essential for managing self-destructive behavior. Individuals can benefit from strategies that help them control emotional impulses and make healthier choices.

Counseling and Therapy: Counseling and therapy can be highly effective in addressing the root causes of self-destructive behavior and developing healthier coping strategies.

Addiction Treatment: Individuals struggling with addiction should seek addiction treatment programs, which offer support and strategies to overcome substance dependency.

Supportive Social Networks: Building and maintaining supportive social networks can help individuals overcome self-destructive behavior by providing understanding, encouragement, and accountability.

Educational Initiatives: Educational programs and campaigns can raise awareness about self-destructive behavior and provide resources for those in need of help.

Legal and Policy Measures: In some cases, legal and policy measures may be necessary to address self-destructive behavior, particularly in areas like substance abuse or self-harm.

Self-destructive behavior is a personal challenge that has profound consequences for individuals, their relationships, their workplaces, and society as a whole.

Mitigating self-destructive behavior involves self-awareness, emotion regulation, counseling and therapy, addiction treatment, supportive social networks, educational initiatives, and, in some cases, legal and policy measures. By fostering a culture of self-care, support, and responsible decision-making, we can reduce the prevalence of self-destructive behavior and work toward a society that is more thoughtful, resilient, and enlightened.

Part IV
Societal Impact

Chapter 10
ID10T$ in the Workplace

As we continue our exploration of ID10T behavior, our journey leads us to a critical and highly impactful arena where this behavior is of significant concern - the workplace. In this chapter, we delve into the profound implications of ID10T behavior in professional settings, the types of workplace foolishness, and the strategies to mitigate these impacts on both individuals and organizations.

Understanding ID10T Behavior in the Workplace

ID10T behavior in the workplace refers to a range of actions and choices that hinder productivity, disrupt teamwork, and lead to negative outcomes for individuals and their organizations. This behavior can manifest in various forms, from chronic procrastination and irresponsibility to a lack of accountability, poor communication, and unethical conduct. Understanding the nature of ID10T behavior in the workplace is essential for addressing its impact.

Types of Workplace ID10T Behavior

ID10T behavior in the workplace encompasses a variety of actions and attitudes that undermine the efficiency and effectiveness of individuals and organizations. Some common types of workplace ID10T behavior include:

1. **Chronic Procrastination:** Individuals who habitually delay tasks, miss deadlines, and fail to complete their work on time create bottlenecks and negatively impact their colleagues and the organization as a whole.

2. **Irresponsibility:** A lack of responsibility is evident when individuals fail to take ownership of their tasks and obligations, leaving

their work unfinished or requiring others to pick up the slack.

3. **Poor Communication:** Workplace ID10T behavior often includes a failure to communicate effectively. This can lead to misunderstandings, misalignment, and conflicts among team members.

4. **Lack of Accountability:** Individuals who shirk accountability for their actions, deflect blame onto others, or avoid taking responsibility for their mistakes can undermine trust and teamwork.

5. **Ethical Lapses:** Engaging in unethical behavior, such as dishonesty, deceit, or harmful actions toward colleagues, damages the ethical integrity of the workplace.

6. **Inefficiency:** Working inefficiently or failing to adopt best practices can lead to wasted time, resources, and opportunities.

7. **Disruptive Behavior:** Disruptive actions that negatively impact the work environment, such as constant complaining, refusal to follow protocols, or excessive distractions, can hinder productivity and morale.

The Impact of ID10T Behavior in the Workplace

The consequences of ID10T behavior in the workplace are profound and extend beyond individual experiences to affect the organization as a whole:

Decreased Productivity: Workplace ID10T behavior leads to decreased productivity, as tasks are delayed, mishandled, or left unfinished.

Missed Deadlines: Chronic procrastination and irresponsibility often result in missed project deadlines, causing delays and potentially harming the organization.

Operational Inefficiency: A lack of efficiency, disruptive behavior, and poor communication can result in operational inefficiencies, affecting the organization's performance and profitability.

Stress and Frustration: ID10T behavior creates stress and frustration for colleagues who must contend with its consequences, potentially leading to decreased job satisfaction and morale.

Conflict and Tension: Poor communication and a lack of accountability can foster conflict and tension among team members, harming the workplace environment.

Reputation Damage: Workplace ID10T behavior can harm an organization's reputation, making it less attractive to potential employees and clients.

Legal Consequences: In some cases, certain forms of workplace ID10T behavior may lead to legal consequences, including lawsuits and fines.

Mitigating ID10T Behavior in the Workplace

Addressing ID10T behavior in the workplace requires a proactive and multi-pronged approach that fosters individual responsibility, teamwork, and organizational values.

Clear Expectations: Organizations should establish clear expectations for employees regarding their responsibilities, performance standards, and ethical conduct.

Effective Communication: Promoting effective communication through training and open dialogue can help reduce misunderstandings and conflicts.

Accountability: Cultivating a culture of accountability is essential. Employees should be encouraged to take ownership of their work and accept responsibility for their actions.

Ethical Training: Organizations should provide ethical training and establish ethical guidelines to ensure employees understand and adhere to ethical standards.

Conflict Resolution: Implementing effective conflict resolution mechanisms can help address disputes and tensions arising from workplace ID10T behavior.

Performance Evaluation: Consistent performance evaluation, feedback, and recognition of contributions can motivate employees to uphold high standards of behavior and productivity.

Mentorship and Training: Providing mentorship and training opportunities can help employees develop the skills and knowledge needed to excel in their roles.

Support for Work-Life Balance: Encouraging a healthy work-life balance and offering support for employee well-being can reduce stress and the likelihood of ID10T behavior.

Legal and Policy Measures: In some instances, legal and policy measures, including codes of conduct, disciplinary actions, and legal consequences, may be necessary to address severe workplace ID10T behavior.

ID10T behavior in the workplace has significant and far-reaching consequences for both individuals and organizations.

Mitigating ID10T behavior in the workplace involves clear expectations, effective communication, accountability, ethical training, conflict resolution, performance evaluation, mentorship and training, support for work-life balance, and, in some cases, legal and policy measures.

Chapter 11
Stupidity in Politics

Our exploration of ID10T behavior now takes us into the heart of political arenas, where decisions made by leaders and the actions of individuals in the realm of politics have the power to shape entire nations and influence the course of history. In this chapter, we delve into the implications of political stupidity, the forms it can take, and the strategies to mitigate its impact on society as a whole.

Understanding Political Stupidity

Political stupidity, in its various manifestations, represents actions, policies, and decisions made by political leaders and individuals that run counter to the best interests of a nation or community. It often involves choices that prioritize short-term gain over long-term well-being, personal ambition over public service, and ideological rigidity over evidence-based governance. Understanding the nature of political stupidity is crucial for comprehending its impact.

Forms of Political Stupidity

Political stupidity can manifest in a multitude of ways within the political landscape. Some common forms of political stupidity include:

1. **Short-Term Populism:** Political leaders may employ short-sighted, populist measures that resonate with the electorate in the short term but prove detrimental to the nation's long-term interests.

2. **Ideological Rigidity:** Rigid adherence to ideological principles, even when they conflict with available evidence or the best interests of a nation, can result in political decisions that are against the common good.

3. **Polarization and Division:** Fostering political polar-

ization and division for personal or party gain can undermine societal cohesion and hinder the ability to address pressing issues.

4. **Corruption and Self-Enrichment:** Political stupidity often involves corrupt practices where leaders prioritize personal enrichment over public service and financial integrity.

5. **Failure to Address Global Challenges:** Ignoring or denying global challenges, such as climate change, can result in a failure to protect a nation's long-term well-being.

6. **Neglect of Healthcare and Education:** Failing to invest in healthcare and education, two cornerstones of a nation's future prosperity, can lead to societal decline.

The Impact of Political Stupidity

The consequences of political stupidity are profound and far-reaching, impacting nations, economies, and societies on multiple levels:

Economic Consequences: Political decisions that prioritize short-term gain over long-term stability can lead to economic crises, income inequality, and a lack of financial security for citizens.

Environmental Damage: Failing to address environmental challenges, such as climate change, can result in environmental damage, including natural disasters, resource depletion, and loss of biodiversity.

Healthcare and Education: Neglecting investments in healthcare and education can result in poorer public health, lower educational standards, and reduced economic competitiveness.

Social Division: Political polarization and division can lead to societal conflict, mistrust, and a failure to address pressing issues.

Erosion of Democracy: Political corruption and self-enrichment can erode the foundations of democracy, undermine public trust, and lead to a disregard for the rule of law.

International Reputation: Political stupidity on the global stage can damage a nation's international reputation, affecting diplomatic relations, trade, and cooperation on global issues.

Mitigating Political Stupidity

Addressing political stupidity requires a comprehensive approach that emphasizes evidence-based decision-making, public accountability, and responsible leadership.

Evidence-Based Decision-Making: Political leaders should prioritize evidence-based decision-making and consult with experts in various fields to inform their choices.

Public Accountability: Public accountability mechanisms, such as transparency, oversight, and checks and balances, are essential for holding political leaders accountable for their actions.

Civic Education: Civic education initiatives can help citizens better understand political processes, critically evaluate political actions, and engage in informed civic participation.

Media Literacy: Promoting media literacy helps individuals distinguish reliable information from misinformation, reducing the influence of sensationalism and propaganda.

Ethical Leadership: Political leaders should prioritize ethical leadership, placing the well-being of their nation and its citizens above personal ambition or party interests.

Civil Discourse: Encouraging civil discourse and respectful dialogue in politics can foster a climate where rational discussions and constructive debates are valued.

International Cooperation: Addressing global challenges requires international cooperation and diplomacy, with nations working together to find solutions to shared problems.

Political stupidity is a complex and pervasive issue that impacts not only individual nations but the global community.

Mitigating political stupidity involves evidence-based decision-making, public accountability, civic education, media literacy, ethical leadership, civil discourse, and international cooperation. By fostering a culture of responsibility, informed governance, and international collaboration, we can reduce the prevalence of political stupidity.

Chapter 12
ID10T$ and the Media

As we continue our exploration of ID10T behavior and its far-reaching implications, we shift our focus to the powerful realm of the media. This chapter gets into the multifaceted relationship between media and stupidity, the ways in which the media can perpetuate foolishness, and strategies to mitigate the impact on individuals and society as a whole.

Understanding ID10T Behavior in the Media

ID10T behavior in the media refers to actions, choices, and practices within the media landscape that prioritize sensationalism, misinformation, or entertainment value over accuracy, truth, and public interest. This behavior can manifest in various forms, from biased reporting and clickbait headlines to the spread of misinformation, fake news, and the glorification of shallow content. Understanding the nature of ID10T behavior in the media is essential for addressing its impact.

Forms of ID10T Behavior in the Media

ID10T behavior in the media encompasses a variety of actions and attitudes that undermine the media's role as an objective and reliable source of information. Some common forms of ID10T behavior in the media include:

1. **Sensationalism:** Prioritizing sensational stories or headlines that grab attention but lack substance, which can lead to a distortion of priorities and public perception.

2. **Bias and Selective Reporting:** Presenting information in a biased or one-sided manner, which can shape public opinion and hinder informed decision-making.

3. **Misinformation and Fake News:** Disseminating

false or misleading information, which can confuse the public and erode trust in the media.

4. **Clickbait:** Using misleading or sensationalized headlines or thumbnails to attract clicks, often at the expense of accurate reporting.

5. **Shallow Content:** Prioritizing entertainment or celebrity news over substantive and informative reporting, which can contribute to societal apathy and superficiality.

The Impact of ID10T Behavior in the Media

The consequences of ID10T behavior in the media are profound and extend to all facets of society:

Erosion of Trust: Sensationalism, bias, and misinformation erode trust in media outlets, leading to public skepticism and decreased reliance on credible sources.

Polarization: Biased reporting and one-sided narratives can fuel political and social polarization, contributing to societal division and conflict.

Misinformed Public: The spread of misinformation and fake news can leave the public misinformed, potentially influencing their beliefs and actions.

Shaping Public Opinion: Media that prioritizes sensationalism and shallow content can shape public opinion based on entertainment value rather than factual accuracy.

Impact on Decision-Making: The media's role in promoting ID10T behavior can hinder rational decision-making, as individuals may prioritize sensational stories over substantive information.

Reputation Damage: Media outlets that engage in ID10T behavior risk damaging their reputation, potentially losing credibility, readership and/or viewership.

Mitigating ID10T Behavior in the Media

Addressing ID10T behavior in the media requires a comprehensive approach that emphasizes ethical journalism, media literacy, and responsible consumption of information.

Ethical Journalism: Encouraging ethical journalism practices, such as fact-checking, balanced reporting, and accountability for errors, is vital for maintaining the integrity of the media.

Media Literacy: Promoting media literacy helps individuals critically evaluate the information they consume, distinguishing credible sources from sensationalized or biased content.

Responsible Consumption: Encouraging responsible consumption of media involves being discerning consumers, seeking out reliable sources, and avoiding the perpetuation of sensational or misleading content.

Transparency: Media outlets should prioritize transparency in their reporting, disclosing their sources, biases, and potential conflicts of interest.

Fact-Checking: Fact-checking initiatives can help identify and correct false or misleading information, holding media outlets accountable for their reporting.

Public Engagement: Encouraging public engagement

with media outlets through letters to the editor, comments, and feedback can foster a more responsive and accountable media.

Media Accountability: Media organizations should establish mechanisms for accountability, such as ombudsmen or public editors, to address complaints and concerns from the public.

Media Diversity: Promoting diversity in media ownership, voices, and perspectives can lead to more balanced and inclusive reporting.

ID10T behavior in the media is a complex and pervasive issue that has profound implications for individuals, society, and democracy as a whole.

Mitigating ID10T behavior in the media involves ethical journalism, media literacy, responsible consumption, transparency, fact-checking, public engagement, media accountability, and media diversity. By fostering a culture of ethical reporting, responsible consumption, and open discourse, we can reduce the prevalence of media-related ID10T behavior.

Part V
Finale

Chapter 13
The Way Forward
and the Media

As we stand at the crossroads of this exploration into the complex phenomenon of ID10T behavior, our journey nears its end, but it is here that our mission truly takes shape. In this closing chapter, we shall chart the path forward, recognizing the pivotal role that the media plays in addressing and mitigating ID10T behavior, while acknowledging the multifaceted effort required from individuals, communities, organizations, and institutions to counteract its pervasive influence.

The Way Forward

The way forward in addressing and mitigating ID10T behavior is not a straightforward, linear path. Instead, it's a collective and dynamic effort that involves a web of stakeholders committed to making a difference. It necessitates a multi-pronged approach, which acknowledges the complexity and pervasiveness of this behavior.

Promoting Education and Critical Thinking

Education is a cornerstone in the battle against ID10T behavior. By investing in educational systems that emphasize critical thinking, problem-solving, and media literacy, we empower individuals to navigate the intricate information landscape with discernment. This extends to media literacy programs that teach individuals how to evaluate sources, fact-check information, and discern sensationalism or bias.

Nurturing Ethical Leadership

Leaders across various domains, including politics, media, business, and community organizations, wield significant influence in setting the tone for responsible decision-making and behavior. Nurturing ethical leadership entails promoting values such as integrity, accountability, and transparency. It also necessitates holding leaders to high ethical standards and rewarding those who prioritize the public good over personal gain.

Fostering Open Dialogue and Diversity of Perspectives

Creating spaces for open dialogue and the free exchange of ideas is paramount in breaking down echo chambers and reducing polarization. Encouraging diversity of perspectives, whether in media, workplaces, or civic spaces, cultivates a richer understanding of complex issues and facilitates the development of comprehensive solutions. Diversity also helps counteract the spread of misinformation and false beliefs.

Media Accountability and Responsibility

Media organizations hold a pivotal role in shaping public discourse and perceptions. Ensuring media accountability and responsibility necessitates adhering to ethical journalistic standards, prioritizing accurate reporting, and correcting errors transparently. Media outlets should be dedicated to the public interest and resist the allure of sensationalism or misinformation for short-term gains.

Fact-Checking and Correction Initiatives

Fact-checking organizations and initiatives should be supported and encouraged. These entities play a vital role in identifying and correcting misinformation and false claims, thereby upholding the integrity of information in the public sphere. Media outlets, organizations, and individuals should also be receptive to corrections and updates.

Community and Civic Engagement

Communities and individuals should actively engage in the political and social processes that shape their lives. This engagement involves participating in local and national elections, supporting civil society organizations, and advocating for responsible governance. Civic participation serves as a potent tool for holding leaders accountable and shaping policies that reflect the public interest.

Responsible Consumption of Information

Individuals have a vital role in mitigating ID10T behavior by being responsible consumers of information. This entails critically evaluating the sources they rely on, cross-referencing information, and exercising caution regarding sensationalism or bias. By seeking out reliable and well-rounded sources, individuals contribute to a more informed and responsible society.

Media Diversity and Pluralism

Promoting media diversity and pluralism is crucial to ensure that a variety of perspectives and voices are represented in the media landscape. A diverse media ecosystem helps counteract the spread of ID10T behavior by providing a range of viewpoints and information sources. Efforts should be made to support independent and diverse media outlets.

Ethical Use of Technology

The responsible use of technology is essential in addressing the spread of ID10T behavior, particularly in online spaces. Individuals and organizations should be conscious of the impact of their online actions, including the sharing of false information, the perpetuation of conspiracy theories, and cyberbullying. Ethical use of technology promotes a more constructive online environment.

Global Collaboration

Many issues related to ID10T behavior, such as climate change and the spread of global misinformation, require international cooperation and collaboration. Nations should work together to address shared challenges and promote a culture of evidence-based decision-making on a global scale.

The Media's Role in the Way Forward

The media plays a pivotal role in the way forward, as it is both a powerful influencer and a critical watchdog. Its influence extends to shaping public perception, setting agendas, and holding the powerful accountable. To fulfill its role effectively, the media must embrace its responsibilities and adhere to ethical standards.

Responsible Reporting

Media outlets must prioritize responsible reporting, which includes fact-checking, transparent sourcing, and ethical decision-making. By providing the public with accurate, well-researched, and balanced information, the media can help counteract the spread of ID10T behavior.

Fostering Media Literacy

Promoting media literacy is a key responsibility for media organizations. By engaging in educational initiatives that teach individuals how to critically evaluate information, media outlets can empower the public to be discerning consumers of information.

Diverse Representation

Ensuring diverse representation within the media is essential. This includes diverse voices, perspectives, and backgrounds. Media outlets should make a concerted effort to reflect the full spectrum of society in their reporting and representation.

Fact-Checking and Accountability

Media organizations should establish robust fact-checking and accountability mechanisms. Corrections and clarifications should be issued promptly and transparently when errors are identified. Accountability measures should extend to addressing issues of bias, sensationalism, and misinformation.

Promoting Civic Engagement

The media can play a pivotal role in promoting civic engagement by covering issues of public concern, providing platforms for informed debate, and encouraging participation in the democratic process. By acting as a bridge between the public and their elected representatives, the media can enhance civic participation.

The journey to address and mitigate ID10T behavior is a multifaceted endeavor that involves education, ethical leadership, open dialogue, media accountability, and responsible consumption of information. It is a journey that requires the commitment of individuals, communities, organizations, and media outlets.

The media's role in the way forward is pivotal. Responsible reporting, fostering media literacy, diverse representation, fact-checking, accountability, and the promotion of civic engagement are all critical functions of the media in addressing ID10T behavior.

In this complex and interconnected world, the battle against ID10T behavior is ongoing. It requires vigilance, education, and a commitment to the responsible use of information.

Chapter 14
The Crusade to Stop
ID10T Behavior

In our journey through the intricacies of ID10T behavior, we've explored the vast landscape of cognitive biases, the perils of impulsivity, and the consequences of a lack of critical thinking and emotional intelligence. We've explored the echo chamber effect and the Dunning-Kruger effect, witnessing how they shape thought patterns and actions. We've uncovered stories that exemplify the real-world impact of these behavioral patterns and the ways in which they can undermine our personal lives, our communities, and society as a whole.

But now, as we conclude this book, it's time to embark on a new phase of our exploration—a call to action. It's time to turn our understanding of ID10T behavior into a crusade to stop it in its tracks, to pave the way for a society that prizes thoughtful, informed, and responsible behavior.

The Power of Self-Reflection

The first step in our crusade is a personal one. It involves looking inwards and reflecting on our own behavior. ID10T behavior is not an affliction that only affects others; it's a malady that can strike anyone. In our fast-paced, information-saturated world, it's easy to succumb to cognitive biases, impulsivity, and the lure of the echo chamber. The key is self-awareness.

Self-reflection is a powerful tool for recognizing and correcting our own behavior. It's about asking ourselves tough questions, challenging our assumptions, and being willing to admit when we're wrong. It's about fostering a growth mindset, acknowledging that there's always more to learn, and that no one has all the answers. By embracing self-reflection, we not only protect ourselves from ID10T behavior but also serve as a model for others to do the same.

Education as the
Light of Inspiration

Education has the potential to be a light of inspiration in our crusade against ID10T behavior. From the earliest days of schooling to lifelong learning, education can instill critical thinking and emotional intelligence as foundational skills. But for this to happen, it requires a transformation in the way we approach teaching and learning.

Educators bear the responsibility of equipping the next generation with the tools they need to navigate the complexities of the modern world. This means going beyond rote memorization and standardized tests to emphasize skills like critical thinking, media literacy, and emotional intelligence. It means fostering an environment in which questions are encouraged, curiosity is nurtured, and the pursuit of truth is paramount.

But the responsibility doesn't rest solely on the shoulders of educators. It extends to parents, guardians, and mentors as well. These individuals play a critical role in reinforcing the values of responsible behavior.

The Fight Against Misinformation

Misinformation, in the age of the internet and social media, has become one of the most formidable adversaries in our crusade. It's a powerful catalyst for ID10T behavior, as it feeds cognitive biases and perpetuates the echo chamber effect. To combat misinformation, we must rely on the pillars of media literacy and responsible consumption of information.

Media literacy is the ability to critically evaluate information, discern credible sources from unreliable ones, and understand the power dynamics that influence media narratives. It's not just about knowing how to fact-check, but also about being aware of the potential biases in the content we consume. The fight against misinformation begins with media literacy education.

One of the most potent tools in this fight is the practice of cross-referencing. When we encounter information, especially information that triggers our emotions or aligns with our existing beliefs, it's essential to seek multiple sources and perspectives. This not only helps us uncover the truth but also breaks down the walls of the echo chamber.

Promoting Responsible Media

The responsibility to combat misinformation doesn't rest solely on individuals. Media organizations, too, must play their part in this crusade. Journalism has a sacred duty to report the truth, and this duty is at the heart of responsible media.

Responsible media involves rigorous fact-checking, transparency in corrections, and the commitment to providing balanced reporting. It means resisting the allure of sensationalism and clickbait and, instead, prioritizing information that serves the public interest. Media organizations must actively engage with diverse perspectives and provide platforms for informed debate.

As consumers of media, we must also hold media organizations accountable. We can do this by supporting quality journalism, subscribing to credible sources, and demanding transparency and ethical reporting.

Navigating the Echo Chamber

The echo chamber effect is a powerful force in ID10T behavior. It reinforces our existing beliefs and isolates us from alternative viewpoints. But, with the right strategies, we can break free from this self-imposed intellectual isolation.

One approach is to actively seek out diverse sources of information. By deliberately exposing ourselves to perspectives that challenge our beliefs, we can become more open-minded and less susceptible to cognitive biases. Engaging in respectful, evidence-based discussions with those who hold different views can also broaden our horizons.

It's important to remember that the echo chamber isn't just about the information we consume but also about the communities we engage with. Social media platforms often curate our feeds based on our preferences, further entrenching us in echo chambers. To counteract this, we can follow individuals and organizations that represent a range of perspectives and interests, ensuring our online experiences are more diverse and thought-provoking.

Encouraging Critical Thinking

Critical thinking is the cornerstone of our crusade against ID10T behavior. It's the ability to evaluate information, identify biases, and make informed judgments. Critical thinking goes hand in hand with a willingness to question our own beliefs and be open to new information.

To encourage critical thinking, we can employ various techniques. We should be cautious of our own cognitive biases, recognizing when they may be clouding our judgment. We can also practice active listening, which involves truly hearing what others are saying before formulating a response.

By seeking out evidence and examining the credibility of sources, we can make more informed decisions and resist the Dunning-Kruger effect.

Generally, and in our educational institutions, we must place a greater emphasis on teaching critical thinking skills. This includes fostering environments in which students are encouraged to question, explore, and think independently. Critical thinking should not be an isolated subject but a thread that runs through all areas of learning.

The Road to Self-Improvement

Our crusade against ID10T behavior is a journey of self-improvement. It's about recognizing our own fallibility, acknowledging our biases, and striving for personal growth. It's a commitment to responsible behavior in thought, action, and deeds.

This journey is not without challenges. It requires patience and perseverance. It means standing up against the current of misinformation and resisting the allure of immediate gratification. But it's a journey worth embarking on, for the destination is a society that prizes wisdom, empathy, and informed decision-making.

Our mission is clear: to be the change we want to see in the world. It's about taking individual and collective action to build a society in which responsible behavior is the norm, not the exception. Together, we can crusade against ID10T behavior, and in doing so, we can shape a brighter future for ourselves and the generations that follow.

The Future Awaits

As we conclude this exploration of ID10T behavior, we do so with a sense of purpose and determination. Our journey has uncovered the pitfalls of thoughtless behavior, the consequences of cognitive biases, and the insidious influence of the echo chamber. But it has also illuminated the path forward—a path of self-reflection, education, media literacy, responsible behavior, and critical thinking.

The future awaits, and it is a future we have the power to shape. It is a future in which individuals are informed, empathetic, and resilient in the face of ID10T behavior. It is a future in which we prioritize truth over misinformation, open dialogue over echo chambers, and responsible behavior over impulsivity.

The crusade to stop ID10T behavior is not a solitary journey; it's a collective endeavor. It's a call to action for individuals, communities, educators, and media organizations. It's a commitment to a society in which thought, action, and deeds are guided by wisdom and empathy.

The road ahead may be challenging, but it is a road worth traveling. For in our crusade, we forge a path to a brighter, more thoughtful future—a future in which ID10T behavior is the exception, not the rule. With determination and resilience, we can make this vision a reality or we could surely perish by our own hands.

The future is here, and the time to act is now.

Let the crusade begin.

Appendix A
Self-Assessment
for ID10T Behavior

This self-assessment is designed to help individuals evaluate their own behavior and identify any tendencies towards ID10T behavior, whether in thought, action, or deeds. The purpose is not to label or judge, but to encourage self-awareness and personal growth. It is important to remember that recognizing areas for improvement is the first step towards positive change.

Please note that the assessment consists of a series of statements, and you are asked to rate the extent to which each statement applies to you on a scale of 1 to 5, where 1 represents "Strongly Disagree," and 5 represents "Strongly Agree." Be honest with yourself in your responses, as this self-assessment is for personal reflection.

Section I
Thought Patterns
1 (Strongly Disagree) 2 3 4 5 (Strongly Agree)

I often dismiss or ignore evidence that contradicts my existing beliefs.

1   2   3   4   5

I tend to believe information I come across online without fact-checking.

1   2   3   4   5

I find myself frequently engaging in "groupthink" and conforming to popular opinions.

1   2   3   4   5

I am generally resistant to changing my mind when presented with new information.

1   2   3   4   5

I often prioritize personal beliefs and emotions over objective facts.

1   2   3   4   5

Section II
Action Patterns

I have a tendency to act impulsively without considering the consequences.

1   2   3   4   5

I often engage in risky behaviors without adequate assessment or precaution.

1   2   3   4   5

Procrastination is a common habit for me, leading to unnecessary stress.

1   2   3   4   5

I frequently make decisions based on immediate gratification rather than long-term goals.

1   2   3   4   5

I tend to neglect important responsibilities and tasks.

1   2   3   4   5

Section III
Deed Patterns

I often find that my actions have unintended negative consequences.

1   2   3   4   5

I sometimes act in ways that harm others without realizing it.

1   2   3   4   5

I have a history of making choices that hinder my own personal development.

1   2   3   4   5

*I frequently engage in behaviors that damage
my relationships with others.*

1   2   3   4   5

*I have a tendency to ignore long-term consequences in
favor of immediate satisfaction.*

1   2   3   4   5

Scoring and Reflection

After completing the self-assessment, calculate your total score for each section by adding up your ratings for the corresponding statements.

Section I
Thought Patterns

Total Score (Out of 25): _____

Section II
Action Patterns

Total Score (Out of 25): _____

Section III
Deed Patterns

Total Score (Out of 25): _____

Now, reflect on your scores in each section. Consider the following:

Are there any particular patterns or trends in your scores?

Are there areas where you have identified room for personal growth and improvement?

What steps can you take to address these areas of concern and reduce the likelihood of ID10T behavior in your life?

Remember that self-awareness is the first step towards change. Recognizing areas where you may exhibit ID10T behavior is an opportunity for personal growth and development. Use this self-assessment as a tool to guide your journey toward more thoughtful, responsible, and informed behavior in thought, action, and deeds.

Appendix B
Resources for Critical Think-
ing and Emotional Intelligence

In our ongoing journey to address and mitigate ID10T behavior, one of the most valuable tools at our disposal is the enhancement of critical thinking and emotional intelligence. These two interconnected skills are essential in navigating the complexities of modern life, making informed decisions, and fostering more thoughtful and informed behavior. This appendix compiles a list of resources that can aid individuals in improving these crucial skills.

Critical Thinking Resources

Books on Critical Thinking

- *Critical Thinking: An Introduction* by Alec Fisher
- *The Demon-Haunted World: Science as a Candle in the Dark* by Carl Sagan
- *Thinking, Fast and Slow* by Daniel Kahneman
- *Superforecasting: The Art and Science of Prediction* by Philip E. Tetlock and Dan M. Gardner

Online Courses and Workshops

- Coursera offers a range of critical thinking courses from top universities.
- edX provides online courses like "Critical Thinking & Problem Solving" from the University of Queensland.

Websites and Blogs

- The Critical Thinking Community (criti-

calthinking.org) offers articles, resources, and teaching strategies.
- The Critical Thinking Project (criticalthinkingproject.com) provides tools for improving critical thinking skills.

Podcasts

- "The Critical Thinking Initiative Podcast" explores critical thinking in education and daily life.
- "You Are Not So Smart" delves into common cognitive biases and misconceptions.

Apps for Critical Thinking

- *Lumosity* offers brain-training games designed to enhance cognitive skills.
- *The Great Courses Plus* features video lectures on various topics, including critical thinking.

Emotional Intelligence Resources

Books on Emotional Intelligence

- *Emotional Intelligence: Why It Can Matter More Than IQ* by Daniel Goleman
- *The Language of Emotions: What Your Feelings Are Trying to Tell You* by Karla McLaren
- *Emotional Intelligence 2.0* by Travis Bradberry and Jean Greaves

Online Courses and Workshops

- Yale University's "The Science of Well-Being" on Coursera covers emotional intelligence and happiness.
- Search for local workshops on emotional intelligence in your area or virtually.

Websites and Blogs

- The Greater Good Science Center (greatergood.berkeley.edu) offers resources on emotional intelligence, empathy, and well-being.
- Psychology Today (psychologytoday.com) features articles on emotional intelligence and personal development.

Podcasts

- "The Science of Happiness" by the Greater Good Science Center explores the science behind well-being and emotional intelligence.
- "The Tony Robbins Podcast" includes episodes on emotional intelligence and personal growth.

Apps for Emotional Intelligence

- *Headspace* provides guided meditation and mindfulness exercises to enhance emotional self-regulation.
- *MoodTools* offers tools for tracking and managing moods and emotions.

Combined Resources for Critical Thinking and Emotional Intelligence

The Harvard Business Review (hbr.org)

This trusted resource offers articles, case studies, and insights on both critical thinking and emotional intelligence in the workplace.

TED Talks (ted.com)

TED features a wide array of talks on critical thinking, emotional intelligence, and related topics. Explore talks by Daniel Goleman, Daniel Kahneman, and others.

Local Workshops and Classes

Many communities offer classes or workshops on both critical thinking and emotional intelligence. Check local listings and community centers.

Universities and Colleges

Higher education institutions often provide courses and programs on these topics. Look for offerings at nearby colleges or universities.

Psychological Associations

National and regional psychological associations often offer resources and workshops on emotional intelligence and critical thinking.

How to Make the Most
of These Resources

Set Clear Goals: Determine what specific aspects of critical thinking and emotional intelligence you want to improve. Setting clear goals will help you choose the most relevant resources.

Schedule Regular Learning: Dedicate time to learning and practice. Consistency is key to developing these skills.

Engage Actively: Whether reading a book or attending a workshop, engage actively with the material. Take notes, ask questions, and apply what you learn in your daily life.

Seek Feedback: Encourage others to provide feedback on your progress. Feedback from peers, mentors, or coaches can be invaluable.

Reflect and Apply: Reflect on your experiences and apply what you've learned to real-life situations. The true value of these skills is in their practical application.

Join Communities: Seek out communities or discussion groups related to critical thinking and emotional intelligence. Sharing experiences and insights with others can enhance your learning.

Measure Progress: Use self-assessment tools to measure your progress over time. This can help you identify areas that need further attention.

Enhancing critical thinking and emotional intelligence is a lifelong journey. It requires dedication, practice, and an open attitude toward personal growth. These skills are not only beneficial in addressing ID10T behavior but also in becoming more effective, empathetic, and informed individuals. Embrace the resources available to you and embark on the path toward a more thoughtful and enlightened self.

Appendix C
Guide to Recognizing
and Addressing
ID10T Behavior

This guide serves as a practical tool to help individuals recognize and address ID10T behavior in thought, action, and deeds. By fostering a deeper understanding of this behavior and offering actionable strategies for tackling it, we aim to empower individuals to become more thoughtful and responsible in their choices and interactions.

Section I
Recognizing ID10T Behavior

Awareness of Thought Patterns

ID10T behavior often starts with flawed thinking. Recognize when you are dismissing evidence, believing information without verification, or engaging in "groupthink."

Identifying Action Patterns

Actions that reflect ID10T behavior include impulsivity, risky behaviors, procrastination, and prioritizing immediate gratification. Be mindful of these tendencies.

Noticing Deed Patterns

Look for unintended negative consequences, harm to others, and behaviors that hinder personal development and damage relationships as signs of ID10T behavior.

Self-Reflection

Regularly engage in self-reflection to assess your behavior and identify areas where you may be exhibiting ID10T tendencies. Be honest with yourself.

Soliciting Feedback

Encourage feedback from trusted friends, family members, or mentors. They can offer valuable insights into your behavior.

Section II
Addressing ID10T Behavior

Embrace Critical Thinking

Cultivate your critical thinking skills by questioning assumptions, evaluating evidence, and considering multiple perspectives before forming conclusions.

Develop Emotional Intelligence

Strengthen your emotional intelligence by practicing self-awareness, self-regulation, empathy, and effective communication.

Practice Mindfulness

Mindfulness techniques can help you become more aware of your thoughts and actions. They can also aid in self-regulation and decision-making.

Fact-Check Information

Always verify the accuracy of information before accepting it as truth. Rely on credible sources and be wary of misinformation.

Seek Diverse Perspectives

Avoid echo chambers by actively seeking out diverse perspectives and viewpoints. Engage in constructive dialogue with individuals who hold different opinions.

Consider Long-Term Consequences

Prioritize the long-term impact of your decisions. Avoid actions that provide short-term gratification at the expense of your long-term well-being or that of others.

Responsibility for Actions

Take responsibility for your actions, especially when they result in harm or unintended consequences. Acknowledge and rectify your mistakes.

Stay Informed

Stay informed about current events, issues, and developments. Being well-informed helps you make more thoughtful decisions.

Resist Impulsivity

When making decisions, resist the urge to act impulsively. Take the time to evaluate your choices and their potential consequences.

Counteract Bias

Be aware of your own biases and work to counteract them. Consider how bias may influence your beliefs and decisions.

Promote Ethical Behavior

Uphold ethical standards in your actions and interactions. Promote honesty, integrity, and accountability in your personal and professional life.

Section III
Engaging Others
in Addressing ID10T Behavior

Lead by Example

Be a role model for thoughtful and responsible behavior. Demonstrate critical thinking, emotional intelligence, and ethical decision-making in your own actions.

Encourage Open Dialogue

Create a space for open dialogue where individuals can discuss their thoughts, opinions, and concerns without fear of judgment.

Educate Others

Share resources and information about critical thinking, emotional intelligence, and responsible behavior with others. Encourage them to educate themselves as well.

Foster Empathy

Promote empathy and understanding in your interactions with others. Encourage individuals to consider the perspectives and feelings of those around them.

Build a Support Network

Establish a support network of individuals who are committed to addressing ID10T behavior. Collaborate to reinforce responsible behavior and decision-making.

Provide Constructive Feedback

Offer constructive feedback to individuals who may be exhibiting ID10T behavior. Do so with empathy and a focus on personal growth.

Contribute to Education

Support educational initiatives that teach critical thinking and emotional intelligence. Encourage educational institutions to prioritize these skills.

Section IV
Ongoing Reflection
and Improvement

Regular Self-Assessment

Continuously engage in self-assessment to monitor your behavior and identify areas for improvement. Adjust your approach as needed.

Seek Professional Guidance

If you find it challenging to address ID10T behavior on your own, consider seeking the guidance of a mental health professional or counselor.

Stay Informed

Stay informed about developments in the field of critical thinking, emotional intelligence, and responsible behavior. Continue to educate yourself.

Promote Positive Change

Advocate for positive change in your community, workplace, and society as a whole. Be a proactive force in addressing ID10T behavior.

Addressing and mitigating ID10T behavior is an ongoing journey that requires self-awareness, continuous improvement, and active engagement with others. By recognizing the signs, actively working to address this behavior, and encouraging responsible behavior in those around us, we can foster a more thoughtful and informed society. This guide provides a roadmap to navigate this path toward enlightenment and positive change.

Appendix D
Interview with Experts

In our quest to gain deeper insights into ID10T behavior and its implications, we reached out to experts in the fields of psychology, sociology, and communication. These experts shared their knowledge and perspectives on the topic, shedding light on the underlying causes, societal impact, and potential solutions related to this behavior.

Interviewee 1
E. Robinson
Clinical Psychologist

Q: From a psychological perspective, what are some of the key factors that contribute to ID10T behavior in individuals?

Robinson: One significant factor is cognitive bias. People often engage in ID10T behavior because they're influenced by cognitive biases that cloud their judgment. Confirmation bias, for example, leads individuals to seek information that confirms their pre-existing beliefs while ignoring contradictory evidence. Similarly, the Dunning-Kruger effect can make individuals overestimate their own knowledge and abilities, leading to poor decisions and actions.

Q: Can you elaborate on how cognitive biases manifest in thought patterns and contribute to ID10T behavior?

Robinson: Certainly. Cognitive biases shape the way individuals perceive and process information. Confirmation bias, for instance, causes people to only consider information that aligns with their existing beliefs. This can lead to the rejection of well-established facts or evidence. On the other hand, the Dunning-Kruger effect can make individuals believe they're highly competent in areas where they lack expertise. This overconfidence can result in reckless actions and decisions.

Q: How can individuals mitigate the impact of cognitive biases on their thought patterns?

Robinson: Developing awareness is key. Individuals can learn to recognize their own cognitive biases and consciously challenge them. Critical thinking, which involves questioning assumptions and evaluating evidence, is a powerful tool in countering these biases. Additionally, engaging with diverse perspectives and being open to new information can help individuals make more informed decisions.

Interviewee 2
M. Sanchez
Sociologist

Q: How does ID10T behavior manifest on a societal level, and what are some of the consequences it may have in the broader community?

Sanchez: ID10T behavior at a societal level often results in the spread of misinformation, polarization, and a decline in the quality of public discourse. When individuals prioritize immediate gratification and impulsivity, they may be more prone to making rash decisions that affect entire communities. This can lead to unintended negative consequences, whether in public policies, environmental issues, or social conflicts.

Q: How can communities and institutions work to address and mitigate the societal impact of ID10T behavior?

Sanchez: Communities can foster a culture of critical thinking and responsible behavior by promoting education, media literacy, and open dialogue. Schools and educational institutions play a crucial role in teaching critical thinking and emotional intelligence. Additionally, fact-checking initiatives and the responsible use of media can help counteract the spread of misinformation.

Interviewee 3
S. Mitchell
Communication Specialist

Q: What role does the media play in either perpetuating or addressing ID10T behavior, and what strategies can media organizations employ to counteract it?

Mitchell: The media wields significant influence in shaping public perception and behavior. Media organizations should prioritize responsible reporting by adhering to ethical journalistic standards, fact-checking information, and transparently correcting errors. Promoting media literacy is another essential strategy. By educating the public on how to evaluate sources and discern bias, media outlets can empower individuals to be more discerning consumers of information.

Q: In an age of rapid information dissemination through social media, how can media organizations combat the spread of misinformation and the echo chamber effect?

Mitchell: Media organizations can take several actions. First, they can dedicate resources to fact-checking and debunking false information promptly. Second, they should avoid sensationalism and clickbait, which can amplify the spread of false narratives. Third, media organizations can actively engage with diverse perspectives and provide platforms for informed debate, thus breaking down echo chambers.

Interviewee 4
D. Carter
Behavioral Economist

Q: From a behavioral economics perspective, how can individuals be motivated to make more thoughtful and informed decisions in the face of ID10T behavior tendencies?

Carter: Behavioral economics suggests that individuals are influenced by both internal and external factors. Nudging, a concept in behavioral economics, involves gently guiding individuals toward better decisions. For example, organizations can implement default options that encourage responsible behavior, making it the default choice. Similarly, positive reinforcement and rewards for informed decisions can motivate individuals to think more critically.

Q: How can organizations and institutions incorporate principles from behavioral economics to reduce the occurrence of ID10T behavior?

Carter: Organizations can apply behavioral economics principles to design decision-making environments that encourage thoughtful behavior. This includes framing choices in a way that highlights long-term benefits, providing clear information, and offering incentives for informed decision-making. By understanding how individuals think and make decisions, organizations can shape the choice architecture to promote responsible behavior.

Interviewee 5
R. Martinez
Media Psychologist

Q: How does media consumption affect individuals' thought patterns and actions, and how can individuals become more discerning consumers of media?

Martinez: Media consumption has a profound impact on individuals' thought patterns and actions. It can shape beliefs, attitudes, and behaviors. To become more discerning consumers of media, individuals should cross-reference information from multiple sources, be critical of sensationalism or bias, and actively engage with diverse viewpoints. Media literacy programs can also teach individuals how to evaluate sources and fact-check information.

Q: What role can media organizations play in promoting responsible media consumption, and what ethical considerations should guide their practices?

Martinez: Media organizations should prioritize responsible reporting by fact-checking information, providing transparent corrections, and avoiding sensationalism. Ethical considerations, such as honesty, integrity, and accountability, should guide their practices. Additionally, media organizations can promote media literacy to educate the public on how to critically evaluate information and sources.

The insights provided by these experts highlight the multi-faceted nature of ID10T behavior and its impact on individuals and society. Recognizing the cognitive biases that contribute to this behavior, addressing it at the individual and societal levels, and promoting critical thinking and emotional intelligence are vital steps in the journey to a more thoughtful and informed society. It is clear that responsible behavior and decision-making are essential for addressing the challenges posed by ID10T behavior in the modern world.

Appendix E
Anecdotal Stories

In the following collection of anecdotal stories, we explore real-life situations that exemplify ID10T behavior. These stories underscore the diverse ways in which thought patterns, actions, and deeds can be influenced by cognitive biases, impulsivity, and a lack of critical thinking or emotional intelligence. While each story is unique, they collectively demonstrate the need for greater awareness and efforts to mitigate ID10T behavior.

Story 1
The Social Media Echo Chamber

Laura, a young professional, had always been interested in politics. She actively engaged in discussions on social media, primarily following and interacting with people who shared her political beliefs. Over time, her social media feed became an echo chamber, filled with like-minded individuals who reinforced her views. Laura rarely encountered differing opinions.

One day, a friend shared a well-researched article that contradicted Laura's beliefs. Instead of critically evaluating the information, Laura dismissed it as "fake news" and unfriended the friend. Her thought patterns had become so entrenched that she couldn't entertain the idea of being wrong. This incident not only damaged a friendship but also exemplified how the echo chamber effect can lead to a closed-minded and unthoughtful approach.

Story 2
The Impulsive Buyer

John, a father of two, was known for his impulsive spending habits. He often made spur-of-the-moment purchases, particularly on items he didn't need. One day, he walked past an electronics store and saw a high-end television on sale. Without considering his budget or discussing it with his family, he bought the TV.

The consequences of this impulsive decision soon became evident. The family's finances were stretched, causing stress and arguments. John had prioritized immediate gratification over his family's financial well-being. This story highlights how impulsivity, driven by a desire for instant satisfaction, can lead to unintended negative consequences.

Story 3
The Procrastinator's Dilemma

Samantha, a college student, was known for her chronic procrastination. Despite her intelligence, she often delayed assignments until the last minute. One semester, she put off a major research project until the night before it was due. Samantha scrambled to complete the project but produced subpar work.

Her professor noticed the lack of depth in the project and asked Samantha to redo it. The consequences of her procrastination included a lower grade, increased stress, and a missed opportunity to learn effectively. This anecdote exemplifies how procrastination, driven by a desire for immediate relief from the discomfort of work, can hinder personal development and academic success.

Story 4
The Biased Believer

Mark had a strong belief in alternative medicine. He frequently visited online forums and websites that supported his views. One day, he came across a story about a person who claimed that a particular herb had cured their serious illness. Mark accepted the story without questioning its credibility or seeking scientific evidence.

He decided to stop his prescribed medication and rely solely on the herb. As his health deteriorated, it became evident that he had fallen victim to the confirmation bias. His strong desire for the herb to be a miracle cure led him to reject medical advice and embrace unverified claims. Mark's story illustrates how confirmation bias can lead individuals to make life-altering decisions based on anecdotal and unverified information.

Story 5
The Shortcut Seeker

David was a business owner who always looked for shortcuts and quick fixes. He often opted for the cheapest, quickest solutions, believing they would save him time and money. One day, his company's IT system was hacked, resulting in data loss and a costly breach.

It was later discovered that David had neglected cybersecurity measures in favor of cheaper alternatives. His pursuit of shortcuts and immediate cost savings had led to severe consequences for his business. This story illustrates how prioritizing immediate gains and disregarding long-term consequences can result in severe setbacks.

Story 6
The Arrogant Expert

Anna, a recent college graduate, had completed a degree in psychology. She considered herself an expert in the field and often corrected people who shared their thoughts or experiences. One evening, she was at a social gathering when a friend began discussing their struggles with anxiety. Anna, convinced she knew everything about the topic, proceeded to offer unsolicited advice and dismiss her friend's experiences.

Her behavior not only damaged the friendship but also exemplified the Dunning-Kruger effect. Anna's overconfidence in her knowledge blinded her to the importance of empathy and emotional intelligence. This story illustrates how a lack of humility and emotional intelligence can hinder relationships and personal growth.

Story 7
The Corporate Short-Termist

Robert was a CEO of a large corporation, known for his obsession with short-term profits. He made decisions that prioritized quarterly earnings, often at the expense of long-term sustainability. This strategy resulted in cost-cutting measures that compromised product quality and employee well-being.

The consequences of his actions became evident when the company faced a series of product recalls and a high employee turnover rate. The pursuit of short-term gains had damaged the company's reputation and long-term viability. This story showcases the dangers of prioritizing immediate financial gains over long-term success and ethical responsibility.

Story 8
The Media Misinformed

Lucy, an avid news consumer, had developed a habit of relying on a single news source for information. She trusted this source implicitly and rarely considered other perspectives.

One day, her trusted news outlet published a sensationalized story without verifying the facts. Lucy shared the story on social media without question.

The story was later debunked, and Lucy faced embarrassment and criticism for her role in spreading false information. Her unquestioning trust in a single source and her failure to critically evaluate the story had contributed to the spread of misinformation. This story emphasizes the importance of media literacy and responsible consumption of information.

Story 9
The Politically Polarized

Jack and Sarah were a married couple with differing political views. Over time, their conversations about politics became increasingly confrontational. They each consumed news from sources that aligned with their own beliefs, further deepening their ideological divide.

The consequences of their polarization were felt not only in their relationship but also in their ability to engage in constructive political discourse. Their unwillingness to consider alternative viewpoints and engage in open dialogue exemplified the impact of echo chambers and the challenges of addressing ID10T behavior.

Story 10
The Environmental
Short-Sightedness

A small coastal town was known for its picturesque beaches and thriving tourism industry. The town council, seeking to boost short-term tourism revenues, approved a plan to build a resort on a sensitive coastal ecosystem. Despite concerns raised by environmentalists and scientists, the plan moved forward.

The consequences were devastating. Within a few years, the ecosystem was irreparably damaged, leading to a decline in tourism and a loss of biodiversity. The pursuit of short-term financial gains had resulted in long-term environmental damage. This story underscores the importance of considering long-term consequences in decision-making.

These anecdotal stories serve as real-life illustrations of ID10T behavior in various contexts. They highlight the consequences of cognitive biases, impulsivity, and a lack of critical thinking and emotional intelligence. Recognizing the diverse ways in which this behavior manifests is the first step in addressing and mitigating it. Through awareness and education, individuals can strive to make more thoughtful and informed decisions in thought, action, and deeds.

Appendix F
Recommended Organizations and Initiatives

As we delve into the task of addressing and mitigating ID10T behavior, it is essential to recognize that no individual or community is alone in this endeavor. Many organizations and initiatives are actively working to promote critical thinking, emotional intelligence, and responsible behavior. In this appendix, we highlight a selection of these organizations and initiatives that individuals, communities, and educational institutions can turn to for support, guidance, and resources.

1. The Critical Thinking Community

Mission: To promote critical thinking in education and society.

Website: www.criticalthinking.org

Description: The Critical Thinking Community provides a wealth of resources, including articles, teaching strategies, and materials designed to enhance critical thinking skills in both students and adults. They offer workshops and professional development opportunities for educators and organizations seeking to foster critical thinking.

2. The Greater Good Science Center

Mission: To promote well-being and emotional intelligence through science-based practices.

Website: greatergood.berkeley.edu

Description: The Greater Good Science Center at the University of California, Berkeley, offers a wide range of resources on emotional intelligence, empathy, and well-being. Their articles, videos, and online courses provide insights into the science of happiness and emotional intelligence.

3. Media Literacy Now

Mission: To ensure media literacy education is included in school curricula.

Website: medialiteracynow.org

Description: Media Literacy Now advocates for the inclusion of media literacy education in K-12 schools to empower students to think critically about media and its impact on society. They offer resources, legislative updates, and guidance for those interested in advancing media literacy education in their communities.

4. The Center for Humane Technology

Mission: To reverse human downgrading and realign technology with human interests.

Website: www.humanetech.com

Description: The Center for Humane Technology, founded by former tech insiders, focuses on addressing the impact of technology on society, including its influence on behavior and decision-making. They advocate for ethical technology design and provide resources for individuals seeking to improve their relationship with technology.

5. The Foundation for Critical Thinking

Mission: To promote educational reform and lifelong learning for critical thinking.

Website: www.criticalthinking.org

Description: The Foundation for Critical Thinking offers books, online courses, and resources for educators, students, and individuals interested in enhancing their critical thinking skills. Their materials focus on principles and strategies for critical thinking and decision-making.

6. The Campaign for Media Literacy

Mission: To promote media literacy and responsible media consumption.

Website: medialiteracy.ca

Description: The Campaign for Media Literacy is a Canadian initiative that advocates for media literacy education and responsible media consumption. They provide resources, toolkits, and information on media literacy initiatives for educators and communities.

7. The Collaborative for Academic, Social, and Emotional Learning (CASEL)

Mission: To advance the science and practice of social and emotional learning.

Website: casel.org

Description: CASEL is a trusted organization that focuses on social and emotional learning (SEL) in education. They offer resources and research on emotional intelligence, empathy, and responsible behavior. Their work supports educators and communities in fostering social and emotional skills in students.

8. The International Fact-Checking Network (IFCN)

Mission: To support fact-checking organizations worldwide.

Website: www.poynter.org/ifcn

Description: IFCN is a global network of fact-checking organizations that promote accuracy in news and information. They provide resources, training, and a code of principles for fact-checkers, media organizations, and platforms to combat misinformation.

9. The Aspen Institute

Mission: To foster leadership based on values, critical thinking, and empathy.

Website: www.aspeninstitute.org

Description: The Aspen Institute conducts research, events, and programs that aim to promote ethical leadership, critical thinking, and empathy. They offer a wide range of resources and events that address societal challenges related to responsible behavior.

10. The Media Education Lab

Mission: To advance media literacy education through research and resources.

Website: mediaeducationlab.com

Description: The Media Education Lab is dedicated to improving media literacy education through research and resources. Their publications, toolkits, and events provide educators and learners with the tools to critically analyze and create media.

11. The Anti-Defamation League (ADL)

Mission: To combat hate and bigotry and promote respectful communication.

Website: www.adl.org

Description: ADL's work centers on combating hate, bigotry, and extremism. They provide educational resources and programs that encourage respectful and responsible communication, critical thinking, and empathy to build a more inclusive society.

12. The National Association for Media Literacy Education (NAMLE)

Mission: To expand and improve media literacy education.

Website: namle.net

Description: NAMLE is dedicated to advancing media literacy education in the United States and beyond. They provide resources, conferences, and support for educators, researchers, and advocates working to promote media literacy and responsible behavior.

13. The International Journal of Emotional Education

Mission: To promote research on emotional intelligence and education.

Website: www.um.edu.mt/ijee

Description: This journal publishes research on emotional intelligence and its applications in education. It is a valuable resource for educators, researchers, and individuals interested in the role of emotional intelligence in personal and societal well-being.

14. The Media Literacy Clearinghouse

Mission: To support media literacy education through resources and information.

Website: www.frankwbaker.com

Description: The Media Literacy Clearinghouse offers a wide range of resources and information related to media literacy and critical thinking. It provides tools for educators, parents, and students to navigate the complex media landscape.

15. The National Council for the Social Studies (NCSS)

Mission: To provide leadership, service, and support for educators in the social studies.

Website: www.socialstudies.org

Description: NCSS offers resources and support for social studies educators. Their materials include strategies for teaching critical thinking, media literacy, and responsible citizenship.

16. The Society for Research in Education and Science (SESES)

Mission: To promote research and education in the fields of science and education.

Website: www.srsd-certificate.com

Description: SESES offers a comprehensive online course called "Self-Regulated Strategy Development (SRSD) Certificate in Teaching Writing." This course equips educators with strategies to teach critical thinking and writing skills.

17. The American Association of Media Literacy Education (AAMLE)

Mission: To promote media literacy education through research and resources.

Website: www.aamle.net

Description: AAMLE focuses on advancing media literacy education and provides resources, conferences, and support for educators and advocates. Their work empowers individuals to critically analyze and create media content.

18. The Journal of Media Literacy Education

Mission: To advance research and practice in media literacy education.

Website: www.jmle.org

Description: This journal publishes research and articles related to media literacy education, critical thinking, and responsible media consumption. It serves as a valuable resource for educators and researchers in the field.

19. The Media Education Research Journal

Mission: To promote research on media education and critical thinking.

Website: www.gala.gre.ac.uk/merj

Description: The Media Education Research Journal publishes research on media education, critical thinking, and media literacy. It is a valuable resource for educators, researchers, and practitioners in the field.

20. The Center for Investigative Reporting (CIR)

Mission: To reveal injustice and hold the powerful accountable.

Website: www.revealnews.org

Description: CIR is a nonprofit newsroom focused on investigative journalism. Their work exposes wrongdoing and promotes critical thinking by providing in-depth, fact-checked reporting on complex issues.

These organizations and initiatives are valuable resources for individuals, educators, and communities striving to address and mitigate ID10T behavior through the promotion of critical thinking, emotional intelligence, and responsible behavior. By leveraging the guidance, tools, and resources they offer, we can collectively work toward a more thoughtful and informed society. Each of these organizations plays a crucial role in advocating for the skills and principles needed to counteract ID10T behavior and foster responsible decision-making in thought, action, and deeds.

Bibliography

1. Baron, J. (2000). Thinking and deciding. Cambridge University Press.

2. Kahneman, D. (2011). Thinking, fast and slow. Farrar, Straus, and Giroux.

3. Tavris, C., & Aronson, E. (2007). Mistakes were made (but not by me): Why we justify foolish beliefs, bad decisions, and hurtful acts. Harcourt.

4. West, R., & Brown, G. (2013). The idiot brain: A neuroscientist explains what your head is really up to. Little, Brown.

5. Stanovich, K. E. (2009). What intelligence tests miss: The psychology of rational thought. Yale University Press.

6. Gilovich, T. (1993). How we know what isn't so: The fallibility of human reason in everyday life. Free Press.

7. McRaney, D. (2013). You are not so smart: Why you have too many friends on Facebook, why your memory is mostly fiction, and 46 other ways you're deluding yourself. Gotham.

8. Paul, R., & Elder, L. (2006). Critical thinking: The nature of critical and creative thought. Journal of Developmental Education, 30(2), 34-35.

9. Dweck, C. S. (2006). Mindset: The new psychology of success. Random House.

10. Sunstein, C. R. (2017). #Republic: Divided democracy in the age of social media. Princeton University

Press.

11. Aral, S., & Walker, D. (2012). Identifying influential and susceptible members of social networks. Science, 337(6092), 337-341.

12. Facione, P. A., & Facione, N. C. (1996). The Delphi Report. California Academic Press.

13. Sagan, C. (1995). The Demon-Haunted World: Science as a Candle in the Dark. Ballantine Books.

14. Fisher, A., & Shapiro, L. (2015). The war on science: Who's waging it, why it matters, what we can do about it. University of California Press.

15. Shermer, M. (2011). The Believing Brain: From Ghosts and Gods to Politics and Conspiracies— How We Construct Beliefs and Reinforce Them as Truths. Times Books.

16. Goleman, D. (1995). Emotional intelligence: Why it can matter more than IQ. Bantam.

17. Brackett, M. A., Rivers, S. E., & Salovey, P. (2011). Emotional intelligence: Implications for personal, social, academic, and workplace success. Social and Personality Psychology Compass, 5(1), 88-103.

18. Strayhorn, T. L. (2014). College students' sense of belonging: A key to educational success for all students. Routledge.

19. Haidt, J. (2012). The righteous mind: Why good people are divided by politics and religion. Vintage.

20. Sunstein, C. R. (2017). #Republic: Divided democracy in the age of social media. Princeton University Press.

21. Head, B. W., & Alford, J. (2015). Wicked problems: Implications for public policy and management. Administration & Society, 47(6), 711-739.

22. Chabris, C. F., & Simons, D. J. (2010). The invisible gorilla: And other ways our intuitions deceive us. Crown.

23. Ariely, D. (2010). Predictably irrational: The hidden forces that shape our decisions. HarperCollins.

24. O'Neill, O. (2002). A question of trust: The BBC Reith Lectures 2002. Cambridge University Press.

25. Tuchman, B. W. (1984). The March of Folly: From Troy to Vietnam. Alfred A. Knopf.

Index

www.ingramcontent.com/pod-product-compliance
Lightning Source LLC
Chambersburg PA
CBHW070329270326
41926CB00017B/3814